Conversations with Emmanuel Levinas,
1983–1994

CONVERSATIONS WITH
Emmanuel Levinas,
1983–1994

MICHAËL DE SAINT CHERON

TRANSLATED BY GARY D. MOLE

DUQUESNE
UNIVERSITY
PRESS
Pittsburgh, Pennsylvania

Copyright © 2010 Duquesne University Press
All rights reserved

Published in the United States of America by
DUQUESNE UNIVERSITY PRESS
600 Forbes Avenue
Pittsburgh, Pennsylvania 15282

No part of this book may be used or reproduced,
in any manner or form whatsoever,
without written permission from the publisher,
except in the case of short quotations
in critical articles or reviews.

Library of Congress Cataloging-in-Publication Data

Saint-Cheron, Michaël de.
  [Entretiens avec Emmanuel Lévinas. English]
  Conversations with Emmanuel Lévinas, 1983–1994 / Michaël de Saint Cheron ; translated by Gary D. Mole.
      p. cm.
  Includes bibliographical references and index.
  ISBN 978-0-8207-0428-9 (pbk. : alk. paper)
  1. Lévinas, Emmanuel. 2. Lévinas, Emmanuel—Interviews.
3. Philosophers—France—Interviews. I. Lévinas, Emmanuel II. Title.
    B2430.L484S24513 2010
    194—dc22
                                                      2009053838

∞ Printed on acid free paper.

In memory of Jack and Ruth Kolbert ז״ל

For Elie Wiesel,
as a token of affection and gratitude,
for his memory, his message,
and the song he passed on to me

For Anne,
without whom this book would not exist

Contents

Translator's Foreword   ix

Abbreviations   xix

Introduction: Decades Attuned to Levinas's Word   1

Part One
Conversations with Emmanuel Levinas: Toward a Philosophy of Holiness

1. Inaugural Meeting, May 9, 1983   13
2. Interviews, 1992, 1994   17

Part Two
From the Phenomenology of the Face to a Philosophy of the Breach

1. From the Epiphany of the Face to the Idea of Holiness   41
2. Sartre and Levinas: Is There a Dialogue?   53
3. Death and the Other or the Dialogue with Malraux   69
4. Otherwise Than Thinking: A Philosophy of the Breach   91

Part Three
Forgiving and the Unforgivable in the Talmud, Based on Levinas's Teaching

1. Yom Kippur, the Day for Forgiveness   113
2. Our Transgressions against Our Fellows   133
3. The Shoah and the Unforgivable   149

Bibliography   162
Index   169

Translator's Foreword

OVER THE LAST DECADE OF HIS LIFE, toward the close of a 60-year career, Emmanuel Levinas agreed to many interviews conducted by diverse interviewers in different contexts, many of which have been collected together by Jill Robbins in her edition of *Is It Righteous to Be?* The present interviews with the philosopher are by no means, therefore, exceptional, but they are *unique,* inasmuch as Levinas is responding to a unique *other*—an*other* face, an*other* voice summoning him to assume that most arduous of intellectual practices Levinas found in the Talmud and in which he delighted: commentary, on his works and thought, his own biography, the philosophical and Jewish traditions, history and politics, the contemporary world around him.

This other voice is that of Michaël de Saint Cheron, known in the wider French academic community for his essays on André Malraux,[1] and in particular for his

---

1. See, notably, his *Notre Malraux* (Paris: Albin Michel, 1979); *Malraux, la recherche de l'absolu* (Paris: La Martinière, 2004); *André Malraux ou la conquête du destin* (Paris: B. Giovanangeli, 2006); and most recently, *Malraux et les Juifs: Histoire d'une fidélité* (Paris: Desclée de Brouwer, 2008). For bibliographical purposes, it should be noted that Michaël de Saint Cheron has published some of his texts under the name Philippe de Saint-Cheron and Philippe M. de Saint-Cheron.

numerous studies of Elie Wiesel, including extensive interviews.[2] The master-disciple relationship in evidence in his interviews with the Auschwitz survivor and Nobel Peace Prize laureate is carried over in the present series of interviews with Levinas, conducted for the most part between 1992 and 1994.[3] While readers familiar with Levinas may not be treated to any startlingly new revelations, Levinas's replies are always characteristically judicious; indeed, Saint Cheron's interviewing technique is not so much to challenge Levinas's discourse—on the contrary, he implicitly endorses most of it—but to encourage precision, even if at times the questions posed have a tendency to break the natural flow of conversation. Certain themes, for instance, are insufficiently teased out, sometimes they are picked up again later, at others they are simply dropped altogether. Yet despite the somewhat

---

2. See, for example, Michaël de Saint Cheron, *Le mal et l'exil: Rencontre avec Elie Wiesel* (Paris: Nouvelle Cité, 1988), translated by Jon Rothschild as *Evil and Exile* (Notre Dame, Ind.: University of Notre Dame Press, 1990); *Elie Wiesel: Pélerin de la mémoire* (Paris: Plon, 1994); *Elie Wiesel: L'homme de la mémoire* (Paris: Bayard, 1998); *Elie Wiesel en hommage*, ed. with Ariane Khalfa (Paris: Cerf, 1999); *Le mal et l'exil: Dix ans après* (Paris: Nouvelle Cité, 1999); and *Entretiens avec Elie Wiesel, 1984–2000, suivi de Wiesel ce méconnu* (Paris: Parole et Silence, 2008).

3. The interviews in part 1, chapter 2, were originally published in Saint Cheron's *De la mémoire à la responsabilité* (Paris: Dervy, 2000), re-edited in a separate volume followed by four essays in *Entretiens avec Emmanuel Levinas, 1992–1994, suivis de Levinas entre philosophie et pensée juive* (Paris: Librairie Générale Française, 2006). This volume was revised by the author with additional new material and published under the title *Entretiens avec Emmanuel Levinas, 1983–1994* (Paris: Librairie Générale Française, 2010). The present translation is based on this revised edition and has incorporated, at the request of the author, other minor changes made to the original French edition.

Translator's Foreword   xi

jumpy nature of the questions and answers, these interviews admirably demonstrate Levinas's ceaseless engagement, right to the end of his life, with what Saint Cheron will call Levinas's "justification for living" after Auschwitz (but also, as is made clear, after Hiroshima, the Gulags, the genocides of Cambodia, Rwanda). This justification, for Levinas, can only be found in ethics, not ethics in the usual sense of moral principles, right conduct or morality—as Levinas himself says here, "It's not because we talk about being selfless and altruistic that we have understood humanity, the other"—but the ethics as first philosophy that questions whether ontology is fundamental, where the other interrupts the self-enclosed totality of being and opens it, infinitely, to responsibility.

Given the period during which the interviews were conducted, it is not surprising that the philosophical domain predominantly under discussion belongs to Levinas's mature and later work. Hence, Saint Cheron invites Levinas to comment in particular on notions such as responsibility, disinterestedness, and holiness as key concepts—though their *saying* exceeds their *said*—to understanding the radical originality of his ethics, but also the much-debated and often misunderstood use of the term "the hostage" in the ethical relation with another person. Other philosophical questions are raised, however, which reflect some of Levinas's earliest preoccupations, notably time and death, with their inevitable inflections in Bergson and Heidegger, but also *Eros* and the feminine, another of the much-contested aspects of Levinas's work. Indeed, it is criticism of Levinas's thought that constitutes one of the interesting issues raised by Saint Cheron, in particular the differences with Paul Ricoeur's own understanding of the other, or with Yeshayahu Leibowitz's stance on ethical relations. Of particular note in the interviews is Saint Cheron's insistence on not only underlining Levinas's proven commitment to Judeo-Christian dialogue in all its urgency after the Shoah and including what Hans Urs von Balthazar has called "post-Christian Judaism," but also highlighting what has been interpreted as the Christian connotations of certain aspects of Levinas's thought. Under discussion too are Levinas's views on the Jewish religious and textual traditions—Torah, the prophets, Talmud—and God himself who, in a striking formulation to which Saint Cheron returns in his introduction, "is not in heaven," but "in the mercy men show for one another." One final topic broached by the interviews, undoubtedly inseparable from Levinas's "break" with the Western philosophical tradition, is history, or rather the momentous and terrible events of the twentieth century which Levinas, born in 1906, had accompanied through to his death in 1995. Having lost the greater part of his own family during the war, it is not surprising that Levinas returns, as he arguably does—implicitly or explicitly—in all of his postwar writings, to the period of the Shoah and its aftermath (here, the Warsaw Ghetto uprising, Polish anti-Semitism, the Touvier affair, or the Carmelite nuns at Auschwitz),[4] but he also responds to questions relating to Communism, Stalinism and the Gulags, and the recent

---

4. Paul Touvier (1915–1996) was head of the intelligence department in the Chambéry militia during the German occupation of France, under the direction of Klaus Barbie. He was finally tried and convicted for crimes against humanity in a much-publicized trial in 1994. Carmelite nuns opened a convent in Auschwitz I in 1984; Jewish opposition led to the agreement of the Catholic Church in 1987 to remove the convent, although it did not actually leave until 1993.

fall, at the time of the interviews, of the Soviet bloc in 1989 with its implications for a renewal of the thought of the Marxist "end of history." Although one can certainly regret that many of these issues are skirted too fleetingly, such as Levinas's views on Zionism, evoked on several occasions, Levinas proves himself, as always, both a tireless provoker of thought and an indefatigable promoter of a post-Auschwitz humanism.

In the five studies that follow the interviews, Saint Cheron takes up and extends a number of questions discussed in the dialogues, but he also raises intriguing issues that have attracted less attention from Levinas scholars. The first and fourth chapters of part 2 are conceptual in nature: Saint Cheron appraises the notion of the epiphany of the face and the idea of holiness in Levinas's thought, following this analysis with a contextualized study of the breach or rupture effected by Levinas in Western metaphysical speculation which for Levinas, from Parmenides through to Heidegger, has always either ignored or harbored an allergy toward the other as other. The focus of Saint Cheron's interest is to trace in Levinas not only the break with the Heideggerian renewal of the question of being—the stage that can be said to begin with *On Escape: De l'évasion* (1935) and to culminate in his first major philosophical text, *Totality and Infinity* (1961)—but also the passage from exteriority and the asymmetry of the intersubjective as analyzed in the rigorous but relatively classical philosophical style of *Totality and Infinity,* to the primacy of the otherwise-than-being in what many consider Levinas's magnum opus, *Otherwise Than Being or Beyond Essence* (1974), with its accent on responsibility and nonthematizable diachrony. For Saint Cheron, however, the final stage in Levinas's mature philosophy is not *Otherwise Than Being,* but the introduction into the strictly philosophical domain of a lexicon more commonly associated with theological discourse: not just revelation and the infinite, already present, for example, in *Totality and Infinity* as central concepts of the interruption of being, but holiness, the holiness of the holy, and in particular God "who comes to mind." It is Derrida who perhaps best summarizes the passage traced by Saint Cheron in these two chapters when in his seminal 1963 study "Violence and Metaphysics" he identifies in Levinas an "ethics of ethics," whereas in his final "Adieu" to Levinas in 1996 Derrida speaks rather of the philosopher's "ethics beyond ethics."[5] It is precisely the path Levinas takes to access the beyond-ethics that Saint Cheron attempts to follow in his investigations into the holiness and the "otherwise-than-thinking" that would characterize Levinas's later work.

The second and third chapters of part 2 are comparative studies organized around, respectively, Sartre and Malraux. Levinas had first written on his illustrious contemporary in 1947, but Sartre had encountered Levinas's name as early as 1930 with the publication of the latter's *The Theory of Intuition in Husserl's Phenomenology*. From this anecdotal opening, Saint Cheron goes on to explore three central issues: first, Saint Cheron offsets the thought of the Other in the respective Sartrean and Levinasian discourses; second, he examines the relatively brief comments that both phenomenologists devote to Kafka and the idea of transcendence; and third, he throws new light

---

5. Jacques Derrida, "Violence and Metaphysics," in *Writing and Difference,* trans. Alan Bass (London: Routledge, 1997), 111; Derrida, *Adieu to Emmanuel Levinas,* trans. Pascale-Anne Brault and Michael Naas (Stanford, Calif.: Stanford University Press, 1999), 4.

Translator's Foreword xv

on how Sartre's controversial final dialogues with Benny Lévy in *Hope Now* (1980), in which Sartre revisits his views on Jews and Jewish history, reflect striking similarities with Levinas's writings on Jewish facticity. In his third chapter, Saint Cheron brings his expert knowledge of Malraux to bear upon Levinas in order to create a fictitious posthumous dialogue between the writer and philosopher, who in reality and a priori seem to have had little to say to each other. Weaving between the moments of epiphany—encounters with death—across a selection of Malraux's novels, memoirs, and television and radio interviews, Saint Cheron subtly and fascinatingly draws out a remarkable and unsuspected proximity of thought between Malraux's own anti-Heideggerian stance and his ceaseless striving to "justify life" in the face of death, injustice, and suffering, and Levinas's thoughts on transcendence and the other. Together, Malraux's staunch agnosticism and the atheism that Levinas's religious philosophy paradoxically courts, offer a profound reflection on fraternity, the absolute, holiness, and the ability to "die for the other."

Part 3, containing Saint Cheron's fifth and by far longest study in the present work, is in a sense the author's most personal homage to his master, offering a reading on forgiveness and the unforgivable in the Talmud that extends in many ways certain motifs of Levinas's own 1963 talmudic reading, "Toward the Other" (*NT* 12–29), but which clearly stakes out his own voice. More expository in terms of Jewish tradition and specifically of the liturgy for Rosh Hashanah, the Jewish New Year, and Yom Kippur, the Day of Atonement, Saint Cheron's essay weaves in and out of the themes of transgression and expiation until its almost inevitable climax with the Shoah through the prism of Simon Wiesenthal's *The Sunflower*, his harrowing 1969 account of his encounter toward the end of the war with a dying SS officer seeking atonement for the atrocities he has committed against the Jews. Saint Cheron's presentation of the dilemma, however, does not stop with Wiesenthal's narrative, concluding his essay with a reflection on some of the Christian reactions to Wiesenthal's text, consonant for Saint Cheron with a scandalously insufficient Christian interpretation of Jewish martyrdom and, as Levinas himself puts it, "useless suffering" (*EN* 91–101).

Levinas's entire ethics as first philosophy is premised on the belief—yet in the light of the massacres and genocides of the twentieth century so much more than a belief—that only the "humanism of the other" can redeem humanity from itself. Saint Cheron's essays are an example of the faith Levinas can inspire in this belief, characterized not by sentiment or some mystical awareness, but by the human *as* other, the reason of history, and the profound conviction that the existence of the divine—regardless of whether or not God exists—is manifested in human and social justice and is absolutely distinct and separate from the "existence of a chair."

To assist bibliographical research, every effort has been made to track down published English translations of texts cited by Levinas and Saint Cheron. When this has proven impossible, or such translations do not exist, I have translated from the French as cited. Some explanatory notes have been added when I thought them necessary or helpful; these are clearly indicated as such. Whenever possible, I have rendered indefinite masculine pronouns (*il, on*) and substantives (*l'homme, le prochain*) with more

Translator's Foreword   xvii

neutral terms in English; when this became too cumbersome, I have sometimes retained masculine forms (*he, man, mankind*), with no gender bias intended. All talmudic extracts and quotations have been systematically checked against the original Aramaic but given as in the Soncino edition of *The Babylonian Talmud*. Biblical quotations are cited as in the *ArtScroll Tanach*, unless part of a talmudic passage, in which case they follow the translation given there. A few inadvertencies and mistaken references have been corrected from the original. Needless to say, all betrayal of the meaning of the original French remains entirely my responsibility.

I would like to thank the author for answering my queries with the utmost courtesy. Thanks are due to all those at Duquesne University Press involved in the production of this translation: Susan Wadsworth-Booth for her managerial efficiency, Brock Bahler for tracking down a few missing references, and Kathy McLaughlin Meyer for her thoughtful copyediting. Finally, I would like to dedicate this translation to my own *others*, Rakefet Shulamit, Pinhas Moshe, and Havatselet HaSharon, for their threefold justification for living.

Abbreviations

The published translations of the following works by Levinas are identified in the text with the abbreviations as indicated. Full bibliographical citations for these titles appear in the bibliography.

AT	*Alterity and Transcendence*
BPW	*Basic Philosophical Writings*
BV	*Beyond the Verse: Talmudic Readings and Lectures*
DE	*Discovering Existence with Husserl*
DF	*Difficult Freedom: Essays on Judaism*
EE	*Existence and Existents*
EI	*Ethics and Infinity*
EN	*Entre Nous: On Thinking-of-the-Other*
GCM	*Of God Who Comes to Mind*
GDT	*God, Death, and Time*
HO	*Humanism of the Other*
IRB	*Is It Righteous to Be? Interviews with Emmanuel Levinas*
ITN	*In the Time of the Nations*
NT	*Nine Talmudic Readings*
OB	*Otherwise Than Being or Beyond Essence*
OS	*Outside the Subject*
PN	*Proper Names*
TI	*Totality and Infinity*
TO	*Time and the Other*

INTRODUCTION

Decades Attuned to Levinas's Word

Since the early 1980s, Emmanuel Levinas's words have been essential to me, as indeed they have for all those who got to know him. From 1983 onward I followed his lessons on Saturday mornings, after the Sabbath service, at the École normale israélite orientale (ENIO) in Paris, rue Michel-Ange. Levinas had been principal of the school for many years before starting a late university career. I remained a faithful participant in these classes right to the end, right to the very last lesson he gave at the beginning of summer 1993. He would give a commentary of the weekly Torah portion read on the Sabbath, which he would enrich with a page from the Talmud. This unforgettable proximity to Levinas's work is one of my two or three major intellectual encounters. As well as providing me with a radically new approach to philosophy, a philosophy that was interested in something other than just Being above everything else, in fundamental ontology, Levinas offered a resolutely "nondogmatic" teaching just as I was taking my first steps in a newly discovered Judaism, in the learning of Torah, the Hebrew Bible, and my discovery of the Talmud, which he defined as an ocean. For all the tiny drops I received, my gratitude toward this master is immense.

Through his work Levinas never ceased responding to the serious question of the defeat of European thought and philosophy, destroyed by Nazi ideology and the destruction of European Jewry but also by Soviet Communism and its own crimes against humanity. If Heidegger proclaimed the end of metaphysics in the classical sense, the metaphysics from Aristotle to Husserl, it was so he could criticize it more effectively for the "forgetting of being" in favor of the first causes of the universe, the principles of knowledge, and the existence of God—or his declared death:

> Does not the true signification of the end of metaphysics, from Kant to Heidegger, consist in affirming that thinking beyond the given no longer amounts to bringing to light the *presence* or the *eternity* of a universe of beings or of secret or sacred principles, hidden in the prolongation of that which is given and which would be the task of metaphysical speculation to dis-cover? Is this sufficient in order to denounce transcendence as non-sense, the very *meta* of metaphysics? And what if its alterity or its beyond was not a simple dissimulation to be unveiled by the gaze but a non-in-difference, intelligible according to a *spiritual intrigue wholly other than* gnosis. (*BPW* 154)

For Levinas, the question of meaning is subordinate to the question of the other, of this "non-in-difference" with respect to my fellow being. Metaphysics thus ceases to be what is beyond physics and becomes what is after being, inasmuch as being is a self, an I, in other words: the other. No longer the primacy of *Dasein,* of being-in-the-world in its *conatus essendi,* its perseverance in being, but the primacy of being-for-others, the being announced by the *Für-Sorge,* the for-the-other.

The interviews the philosopher granted me from 1983 onward, followed by the four essays that extend them and the study on forgiveness in the Talmud from the perspective of Levinas's own writings, throw light on the paths taken by this unclassifiable thinker, at once demanding and generous, whom we could hardly follow with impunity over almost a quarter of a century.

How did Levinas make the move from ethics as "first philosophy" to holiness, a word that arouses fear and to which I shall return? A holiness outside any idea of religious faith, of "revealed" transcendence, being its own form of transcendence. And how, moreover, did he get from the "God who comes to mind" through the face of the other person to the definition of a nonreligious transcendence? The present work attempts to reply to these questions, through, on the one hand, my interviews with the philosopher, and on the other the imaginary or real dialogues with the works of Sartre and Malraux, and even more so with Kant, Heidegger, Nietzsche, or Derrida, as well as the long text on the problematics of forgiveness in the Jewish conscience in line with the texts of midrashic and talmudic tradition.

Among contemporary philosophers Emmanuel Levinas's work has remained in the margins of all the major trends: existentialism, deconstruction, Marxism, structuralism, anthropology, political theory. The same holds in relation to Adorno and Habermas, but also to Hannah Arendt, who all largely ignored him, and again to French philosophers from Foucault to Deleuze, not to mention American philosophers like Rawls. No doubt Merleau-Ponty, Ricoeur, Derrida—who gave his moving speech, "Adieu," at Levinas's funeral at the Pantin cemetery one glacial morning in January 1996—the later Sartre, Lyotard too, and in the current generation Finkielkraut and Jean-Luc Marion, all showed an interest in the work of this philosopher, atypical and yet central to contemporary philosophy. But how many German or Anglo-Saxon philosophers have shown an interest in Levinas?

Paul Ricoeur, in a conversation I once had with him, talked about his proximity to and differences with Levinas. In his book *Oneself as Another,* Ricoeur develops a new ethics by crossing

> the Husserlian line with the Levinasian line, with the conviction that the problem is one of reciprocity which, in my opinion, neither Husserl nor Levinas completely assumed. You probably noticed, moreover, that on this occasion I'm trying to reinvigorate a concept from Hegel, above all the Hegel of the philosophy of Iena, the idea of recognition and mutual recognition, it's precisely this mutuality in recognition that was important to me. Maybe it was necessary to start from two forms of dissymmetry—the dissymmetry me-you in the sense of knowledge, and the dissymmetry you-me in the ethical order—in order to understand through this crossed dissymmetry as it were, mutuality and reciprocity, and by so doing, I would say, tear this concept of mutuality from its banal status, make it more dramatic and more problematic in a certain sense, so as to conquer it with all one's might rather than taking it as is in daily experience, hardly attentive to the paradox already present in the exchange of personal pronouns.[1]

---

1. Saint Cheron, "Entretien avec Paul Ricoeur," 22.

For Ricoeur there is no such thing as a one-way ethics, to think myself uniquely as the other's hostage without any form of reciprocity is to underestimate the other's importance. For the philosopher of *Time and Narrative*, this double dissymmetry is present from the very foundation of my relation with the other. But there is something irreducibly true, namely that Levinas's philosophy is "a philosophy of excess and hyperbole," as Ricoeur himself pointed out to me. Levinas called this excess love, and this hyperbole holiness. He was possessed, as if haunted, by a love that could go so far as to "die for the other," and he criticized Heidegger precisely for refusing the "dying for the other" (*EN* 215) the ability to free the other from dying. Some of Levinas's Jewish readers judged him to have given a seriously Christian interpretation to traditional Jewish teaching through his philosophical and theological conception of sacrificial responsibility, despite the fact that Levinas was no theologian! I wrote to him one day, at the beginning of our friendship, asking him for the Jewish biblical sources of the womb-like mercy[2]—*rahamim* in Hebrew—that can be understood as a "dying for." He wrote back with these magnificent lines:

> Indeed, that love should be stronger than death—and that there is no stronger love than that which leads to dying for another person—I can learn this from the conduct of Queen Esther willing to sacrifice herself for the life of others (Esther 4:16), that is if I'm not satisfied drawing such truths from the Song of

---

2. [Saint Cheron actually writes "miséricorde matricielle," reinforcing the link between the word for "mercy" in Hebrew, *rahamim*, as he points out, and its root *rehem*, meaning womb.—Trans.]

Songs 8:6 where love is only as strong as death and not stronger than death! But that doesn't mean I've overcome the differences separating two great spiritualities nor decided which has priority or which is secondary.[3]

Let me recall finally that Levinas remained vigilant to the end in the dialogue with Christianity, refusing to accept those discourses that while apparently engaging in dialogue with Jews merely seek to seduce them through a thinly veiled, philosophically coated Christian message, though this in no way prevented him, quite the contrary, from being a fervent supporter of Jewish-Christian dialogue, as long as it was devoid of pretense.

The following lines which Levinas wrote to me, again from the year 1983, after I had sent him two articles by Olivier Clément, strongly reflect his position:

> Even though here too it is suggested that the ethical spirit in crisis needs to be rebalanced in a Christian, painless, miraculous if not magical way; that the crisis is the permanent surprise of the spirit; that the spirit's authenticity is achieved only through its effort to seek and take hold of itself as it falls, which would be its very positivity; that the spirit is unceasingly pulling itself together, if not eloquently preaching a sermon; and that time has to be left in this exercise of the spirit for it to recover. Christianity would grant itself centuries to accomplish this, and the count's not yet at an end. But I was very touched by what Olivier Clément says on a number of points and I don't just mean the friendly terms in which he speaks of me.[4]

---

3. Unpublished letter to the author, dated September 6, 1983.
4. Unpublished letter to the author, dated July 22, 1983.

These letters testify to the height at which Levinas permanently placed himself as a man of thought and dialogue, daring to open the philosophical field to the word of the prophets, similar to the way Saint Augustine and Thomas Aquinas had introduced the Christian word above that of Plato and above all Aristotle in the great debate between reason and faith, turning them both, despite themselves, into the two giant precursors of scholastic philosophy. Do the sworn enemies of Levinas's thought reproach him, in the end, for not yet being canonized or worse, for having had the impertinence to grant the right of residence to the prophets of Israel who preceded the fathers of Western philosophy by several hundred years and who for 3,000 years have made heard a word of justice and transcendence, challenging philosophical speculation's claim to it, even if it is that of the Greeks?

In this year of 2006 marking the centenary of Emmanuel Levinas's birth, I can only conclude by repeating the words of General de Gaulle—whom the philosopher moreover admired—written to André Malraux in 1958 after reading *The Metamorphosis of the Gods:* "Thanks to you, I have seen—or thought I have seen—things that otherwise I would have died without even suspecting their existence. And of all things they are precisely those that matter most."[5]

More than a philosopher, Levinas was a conscience, and his discourse, heavily imbued with the spiritual and philosophical values and traditions of the West, carries within it, beyond the concepts of being and nothingness, time and death, even transcendence and metaphysics, the question of the justification for human life. Levinas will

---

5. Quoted in Cazenave, ed., *André Malraux,* 213.

have taught us to recognize this "God who comes to mind," even in agnosticism and atheism. Brought up from an early age on the great novels of Dostoyevsky and Tolstoy, the observant Jew from Lithuania will have taught us to distinguish once more between what is essential and what is secondary in all true spirituality. He was not afraid to exclaim, one Sabbath in the synagogue of the ENIO, before the Holy Ark containing the Torah scrolls, that heaven was empty but that one person's forgiveness of another was filled with God. God was not in heaven, he added, but in people's sacrifice and responsibility for each other.

As a Jew after Auschwitz, conscious of this nontransferable responsibility for having survived six million of his brothers and sisters, his ceaseless metaphysical questioning of humanity's relationship to God, and above all the victim's relationship to God, took on a paradigmatic dimension. There are no sermons possible after Auschwitz, he thought, while warning against considering "Revelation [as] the love of the other man" as "new proof of the existence of God" (*GCM* 168).

His ethics was fundamentally an ethics of temporality, hence his proximity with Bergson. He will have allowed us to understand the cardinal thought of thinking "death on the basis of time, and no longer time on the basis of death" (*GDT* 104).

Let us be attentive then to this philosophical word bearing a future, bearing life and above all bearing the dimension of love, so rare in philosophy, if not to say neglected, indeed deformed, but a "love without concupiscence" cherished by Pascal, a love of the soul calling for transcendent communion. A universal and utopian word par excellence—beyond all forms of hatred of the other, all fanaticisms, all the crises of humanity's folly—for which "the only absolute value is the human possibility of giving the other priority over oneself" (*EN* 109), as Levinas wrote in *Entre Nous,* a text he would have liked to have entitled *After Me.* In this century opening *after him*—in these inhuman times, these times of "the barbarism of being" (*EN* 187)—Levinas's mad utopia of having wanted to believe in the irreducible possibility of the human being to choose holiness is testimony to an inordinate hope in humanity's capacity "to infinitely go beyond the human."

PART ONE

*Conversations
with Emmanuel Levinas:
Toward a Philosophy
of Holiness*

1
Inaugural Meeting, May 9, 1983

Q.: THE CHURCH, OR CHRISTIANITY IN GENERAL, has been teaching for 2,000 years, until recently, that since Christ Judaism, the Synagogue, has contributed nothing new. Is this not contradicted by the evidence given by the whole of twentieth century history, with its nameless tragedy and its intellectual, philosophical, spiritual, and indeed political renewal?

E.L.: But we can already say that the entire reading of the Torah is an incessant renewal, through the study and commentaries that arise from it. It's a *hidoush,* as we say in Hebrew. Your question is the old Judeo-Christian discussion whereby the Jews would have ceased before Christ. But what I remember, in an article on my work you gave me, and I thank you for doing so, are the words of the great German theologian Hans Urs von Balthasar, who wrote that the only viable interlocutor for Christians was "post-Christian Judaism," which he qualified as the "only partner worthy of being taken really seriously." The article quotes a Spanish theologian who wrote a book[1] on my last few works, and which employs the word "syntony." The use of this word insists on the common tonality between Jews and Christians. From our point of view, it's also the idea that Jews don't have anything less than what Christians have, but that we see the revelation in a different way.

Q.: Let me read to you what you wrote in *Difficult Freedom* concerning a text by Stanislas Fumet on the book by Father Menasce,[2] *Quand Israël aime Dieu* [When Israel loves God]: "Certainly we cannot ask a Catholic to 'put away his Catholicism,' but we should despair of humanity if its highest life forms could not assure men of a true contemporaneity. The possibility of a fraternal existence—that is to say, one that is precisely synchronic, without any 'underdeveloped' or 'primitive' peoples—is perhaps the decisive test of the spirituality of the spiritual" (*DF* 130).

E.L.: I am not questioning this text, but the word "synchronic" here is not a term I would employ today. Synchrony signifies that there is nothing left behind. It not only negates the past, it negates the future too. It is in this sense that I would use the term a lot less in our context.

Q.: I recently discovered a passage by Martin Buber in his *Autobiographical Fragments,* in which he recalls

---

1. Vázquez Moro, *El Discurso sobre Dios en la obra de Emmanuel Levinas*. The theologian writer analyzes Levinas's work as a fundamental theology, belonging to "post-Christian Judaism."

2. [Jean de Menasce (1902–1973), Dominican priest, born to a Jewish father in Alexandria, converted to Catholicism in Paris in 1925, one of the leading postwar Orientalists and proponents of Jewish-Christian dialogue.—Trans.]

the episode where Saul sees himself disowned by Samuel—and by *HaKadosh Baruch Hu,* the Holy One, blessed be He—for having left Agag alive. Buber's fierce opposition to Samuel is such that he writes, "Samuel has misunderstood God.... Nothing can make me believe in a God who punishes Saul because he has not murdered his enemy."[3] The question is a serious one and is posed in all its gravity and drama. According to you, can ethics lead us to believe that certain characters in the Bible have misunderstood the divine word, such as Joshua, Samuel, David, or even Elijah?

E.L.: First, I don't believe that one can kill like this face to face as easily as Samuel does. There are definitely certain things in the Bible that shock us, and I think that one shouldn't start with these. But even in these texts, you need to listen to what they are saying. Agag is advancing, he thinks that the severity of death, the "bitterness of death," has left him. Samuel kills him, but before he does so, he says to him, "Just as your sword made women childless, so shall your mother be childless among women!" (1 Sam. 15:32–33). And so your mother shall be childless. The Hebrew has a word lacking in the French, the word *harev* [literally, sword], meaning desolate, in ruins, to speak of the mothers whose children are killed.

So I think one needs to read the text differently from how Buber reads it. Buber wants to be more charitable than Samuel.

Q.: In your opinion, is there not a danger in political Zionism of putting the state above the universal values of the Torah?

---

3. Buber, *Meetings: Autobiographical Fragments,* 63–64.

E.L.: Anti-Semitism is more dangerous than Zionism (laughter). But Zionism can be led astray, there's no denying it.

Q.: How do you conceive of your relationship to God, if I may venture such an intimate question?

E.L.: Listen, God is not in heaven. He is in men's sacrifice, in the mercy men show for one another. Heaven is empty but men's mercy is filled with God.

2
Interviews, 1992, 1994

Q.: How would you define the philosopher's responsibility in the midst of the planetary upheaval we are living through?
E.L.: It's a difficult question, because it would mean that not all people have the same responsibility. I don't believe at all that as a philosopher one is exempt from telling the truth. But if telling it is all well and good, no doubt one has to think sometimes of all the harm that the truth can bring about.
Q.: You have written that ethics is not a branch of philosophy but the first philosophy. When these words are quoted, certain philosophers object by saying that this "disinter-estedness" toward self and the interest in the other are nothing but another form of self-interest, a sublimated egoism, if you like. What is your reply to this criticism?
E.L.: This is in keeping with the history of holiness. Holiness is the responsibility I'm talking about. The reasons why we don't see it through, why we build states,

why we have an ethics limiting this sacrifice, probably come from our infidelity to our moral condition. Not that we don't manage to come to an understanding, but the sacrifice is always incomplete. Perhaps in the concept of holiness there is a place for a concept of the political. Politics derives from the fact that humanity exists, that the exercise of holiness cannot be achieved in intimacy but in multiplicity.

This "dis-inter-estedness" toward the other can thus also be to the disadvantage of a third. Pure holiness, therefore, is possible only in a humanity in which two people exist. As soon as there are three of us, there's the state, because the state is not a pure negation of the moral code. In European law, for example, there is the concern for public morality. Charity and the respect for the other do not exclude the problem of justice.

Q.: How would you define holiness?

E.L.: Good and evil exist together. Let me explain. To accept holiness is certainly to achieve something positive, but on the other hand this positive element is really *nothing* at all, in the sense that nothing is gained.

Q.: So is it a loss?

E.L.: Yes. But it's very dangerous because as soon as you say loss, you are implying it's empty. Whereas for me, this is the only condition that is still Good and already despair, already *nothing*. It's a difficult thing to say. Ultimate holiness is the acceptance of justice or death without resistance, accepting this nothingness and yet nevertheless having this reflex of goodness, of value. Holiness is not in the category of moral things. Why in our liturgy do we say *kadosh,* holy, three times? Because if the first *kadosh* is nothing, then there's the second, and if the second is nothing, there's still the third. It's not at all as if there were three types of holiness, there's only one holiness, but this increase in holiness has to be pronounced as soon as it is refused.

Q.: At the time of the Touvier affair, how did you judge the behavior of the Church in France, directly implicated by the fact that many members of the clergy had hidden him?

E.L.: All I know and what I can tell you is that there are some cardinals who are God's children, like Cardinal Decourtray.[1] The Touvier affair only confirmed my admiration for him.

Q.: Still, one can hardly forget a certain complicity of the Catholic Church in seeking to protect the perpetrators of crimes against humanity...

E.L.: My Judaism isn't shaken for all that. Despite everything, I admire the Church, which means I admire Decourtray.

Q.: I would like to broach with you some of the big questions of the end of the century. There are some eminent scientists who would have political leaders understand that without them, they will be able to do nothing to eliminate the dangers threatening humanity. What do you think of that?

E.L.: It's quite true. In my opinion, what is most dangerous is not so much the atomic bomb falling into other hands, but those scientists who emigrate, what's called the brain drain. Countries like Iraq or Libya use these experts to build bombs. Tomorrow these countries will have the atomic bomb like one has a revolver.

Q.: The great shock of the early 1990s is the collapse of Communism. You yourself were born in Lithuania in 1906 and you personally witnessed the Revolution of 1917. What is your analysis of this event?

---

1. [Albert Decourtray (1923–1994), former archbishop of Lyon, notable for his constant dialogue with the Jewish community, and in particular for opening up to historians the archives of the Diocese of Lyon concerning the period of the Occupation.—Trans.]

E.L.: What's dramatic is that the end of Communism is the temptation of a time that has lost its orientation. We've become so used to considering time as going somewhere, whether it's waiting for the Messiah, waiting for Christ to return, or the movement toward a just society, with this just society oriented toward the end of history. Since Marx, this wasn't what Soviet Russia represented for everybody, but for a part of humanity in any case, the collapse of Communism can be felt as the end of history. Which is why what happened in Russia should not be taken lightly. We have suddenly entered a time that's going nowhere. Either it's good or it's bad, since nothing has meaning anymore.

I can sum this up in a sentence: what time is it?

Are we at the end of history or before the end of history? This is a valid question no doubt for those who never believed Communism to be the end of history and for those who said on the contrary that it was the abnegation of humanity. Ever since the eighteenth century we were living in a rational time, in a time moving toward progress, and progress had become the just society of Hegel and Marx. And here we are today with the impression that time is going nowhere. In other words, it's not sure that we were heading toward what was best. But it's very difficult to put this idea forward, because you're immediately taken for a Bolshevik. I'm not saying I'm a Communist, on the contrary. But when Marchais[2] used to speak in Brezhnev's time, people paid attention to what he said, but then suddenly, when he started talking after

---

2. [Georges Marchais (1920–1997), general secretary of the French Communist Party from 1972 to 1994.—Trans.]

the breakup of the empire, he no longer made any impression at all. What I'm saying is that humanity is asking what time it is. As if all the clocks had been dismantled. And even today, all previsions have been taken apart.

Q.: Auschwitz, Hiroshima, the Stalinist regime: for you, who witnessed these three central events unfold in our terrible twentieth century, what has been their lesson for your thought?

E.L.: That secular messianic ideas are no longer possible because people thought that these events announced the end of history.

Q.: Do you think that the end of Communism and the breakup of the Soviet empire can give new impetus to Zionism?

E.L.: The Zionist problem does indeed take on a lot more meaning at the present time, due to the collapse of the USSR, and above all to the possibility somewhere of a Le Pen.[3] During the glorious era of Soviet Russia, the Zionists were considered small-minded: here we are changing the world order and they still want Mount Sinai!

Q.: In a conversation I had with Paul Ricoeur, he mentioned his debt to you and at the same time the slight difference in his ethical philosophy as regards your own.

E.L.: As you know, I greatly admire Paul Ricoeur. In the whole of contemporary philosophy, he has an audacious and perfectly honest mind. But there's a small disagreement between us on good relations with others. For my part, I have always tried to look beyond the human

---

3. [Jean-Marie Le Pen (born 1928), founder and president of the French right-wing and nationalist party, the National Front.—Trans.]

relations that are well apportioned—and it's already absolutely fortunate if the relations between humans are well apportioned—for the profound foundation that makes the interhuman relation ultimately possible. A relation that is absolutely disinterested. I'm looking for a relation in which my obligation, my awakening toward the other, my attachment to the other are not in any way an attachment or a form of generosity that brings a reward. Which is why I have always thought there was an element of total gratuitousness in the relation to the other, an absolute disinterestedness, and I have come to contest the very reciprocity of the good that appears in this relationship. Paul Ricoeur follows me on a lot of points, but here he believes that the suppression of reciprocity is to lack something, that there's a kind of injustice committed against oneself in this way of thinking. I perfectly understand his reasons, but I thought precisely that at the basis of the pure relation, of the generosity toward the other, there's a relation that one can call a relation of holiness. As if holiness were the supreme dignity of the act of the relationship with the other, what one calls love or respect of one's neighbor.

Paul Ricoeur's critique is to ask why we should deprive ourselves. Why should there not be any ultimate satisfaction in this relation, something other than a pure and simple expenditure?

I think the notion of holiness is unlike any other relation; it has a dignity unto itself. Indeed, holiness excludes all interest. But it's the only gratuitousness that, despite everything, is unique in its kind: it is a value. If holiness is thoroughly analyzed, there really is nothing, but it is precisely this capacity to bear the nothing and to want to bear it that is already a positive quality. The person who is capable of holiness in disinterestedness and who holds steady, despite everything positive that holiness brings, is one of a kind.

Q.: What disturbs Paul Ricoeur and what is difficult for us all to understand, is when you go so far as to say that "I am the other's hostage." "Hostage" is a terrible word.

E.L.: Yes, indeed, this expression means that there are hostages and that one can accept the condition of being a hostage. So this means that my responsibility for the other goes so far as to bear the injustice entailed by the hostage's condition as such. This condition brings something to the other, but it's an acceptance that here again bears witness precisely to holiness. This is all one criticism for Ricoeur. Obviously, willingly accepting the hostage's condition is an act of holiness, even if you give it other names. It's self-evident that holiness is to approach God; it's much more than the so-called glorious visions of God. This concept of the hostage is certainly a peculiar way of promising happiness to the righteous.

Q.: But how do you situate the word as regards talmudic and midrashic Jewish thought?

E.L.: I've been familiar with the word "hostage" ever since the period of Nazi persecution. In making you a hostage, you were being punished for someone else. For me, the term has no other meaning, except when the context gives it a meaning that can be glorious. The misery of the hostage is glorious in a certain sense, to the extent that the hostage knows he is running the risk of being killed for someone else. Yet is there not, beyond dramatic destiny, a supreme dignity in this hostage's condition, what I call the "hostage's uncondition"?

Q.: Is it a dignity that should be sought after?

E.L.: I always insist in my reasoning on the fact that this hostage's condition is the very possibility in the world for pity, compassion, solidarity. There's always a risk of becoming a hostage when one tells the truth. It's a word I use too to express human holiness. The word "holiness" is more flattering than the word "hostage."

Q.: Nevertheless, do you not see in the word "hostage" a specifically Christian connotation?

E.L.: No more so than in the word *kedousha*. I don't know what the Hebrew word would be to designate the hostage. But for me, as I said, it's first and foremost a word I know from the German occupation of Europe.

Q.: It's not a word found in the Torah.

E.L.: In any event the notion of dying for the Name of God is frequent in the Jewish Bible. And didn't Esther run the risk of assuming the hostage's condition to save her people, since whoever approached the king without him first extending his scepter risked death?

Q.: Certain Jewish thinkers say that you give holiness a dimension that isn't Jewish but Christian. What is your answer?

E.L.: You know that in the Hebrew language the word *kadosh* is applied to God, who is *kadosh*, holy, but it can also be applied to men, the *kedoshim,* the saints or holy men. It's an ancient tradition going back to the period of the Talmud. Unless one presumes there is no charity in Judaism, only justice. The liturgical expression *hessed shel emet,* the love of truth, is charity. What is entirely original with holiness—beyond its many other qualities—is also its greatest misery. It's the strength to want what is good for the other in the misery that can come from him.

Q.: George Steiner writes that "Jewish destiny, Auschwitz included, turns around the Epistle to the Romans in which Paul says that the Jew, in refusing to accept the Messiah, holds man a hostage to history." Is this not an outrageous claim?

E.L.: In that case, the refusal to acknowledge Jesus can be understood as being willing to die for the Messiah. Yet the Messiah has no need for it. There are certainly times in Judaism when we encounter this willingness *to die for,* as we have just seen with Esther who risks her life to save her people.

Q.: But not for the Messiah?

E.L.: No, on the contrary. It's not a positive quality of the Messiah who can divert our willingness to die for him. Perhaps Steiner means that suffering is good, in that the Messiah can finally be acknowledged. Unless it's just a fancy on his part.

E.L.: There's a text in the Talmud that says that God plays with the Torah. How do you read this text?

Q.: When the Talmud says that the Torah fell into Moses' hands, we can certainly read it as God playing with the Torah. The way the *Hakhamim,* the Sages, comment on the Torah is a lot like a game. God plays with the Torah by observing the way the experts play with it. When Satan went to look for the Torah, it was in neither the sea, nor the fire, nor heaven. In reality God had given it to Moses and Moses had understood perfectly that it hadn't been given to him but that God was playing with it. So when Satan comes to ask Moses, "Do you have the Torah?," he replies, "God has it." Which boils down to saying that when the Jews have the Torah, God has it. And when God has it, it means that the Jews in the *yeshivot,* the talmudic schools, are weighing it up and commenting on it. It's in the *yeshivot* that God takes delight....

What is interesting in the page I'm referring to in the Tractate Shabbath [89a], is the threefold appearance of the elements. Satan first looks for the Torah on earth, then in the oceans, and finally in the deep. When you haven't studied chemistry or physics yet, water, flames, and nothingness, the *tohu vabohu,* don't belong to the physical order at all. What was the use of the elements before the exact sciences? Our world has analyzed fire, water, the elements, to do chemistry and physics with them. But as soon as there are living beings who work and study, it's the Torah that teaches them how they should work, how they should marry, how they should study.

Q.: Isn't what is important for you the idea that in the Torah God descends to humanity, that his *Shekhinah,* his presence, resides among human beings?

E.L.: Not that he descends, but as if he were to descend. Rabbi Akiba says that the Torah is alive. It's the idea that the only thing that amuses the good Lord is the *yeshiva,* the word...

Q.: Is death conceivable, in philosophical terms?

E.L.: Initially one says that death is negation. But it's not a negation, since it's a mystery. It's not at all that there's no life after death, that there's no hope for survival, for resurrection. The resurrection also says too simplistically that death is nothing. What it is, we simply don't know, because it's a mystery par excellence. To speak of death is to abandon all logic. It's not just a question of the fact that we die. All the logical forms we would use to circumscribe death disappear in the event we're trying to describe.

When we say "He's dead," there's no longer any "he" precisely. As a result we've said nothing when we say, "he's stopped living. It's over." It's not over at all. It's just that here, it's over, there's no more here, there's the nothingness afterwards. And the nothingness afterwards is a nothingness of someone who's been granted an extension. This is not really how consciousness disappears. At what point does it disappear? When I say that death is not nothingness, I'm in no way implying an opposition between being and nothingness. Not that there is an excluded third party, but *as if there were* an excluded third party. To think nothingness and not being is not the same thing. The excluded third party is: there is A and *not* A. Our logic is a logic of the excluded third party.

Q.: Is death, finally, for you, the "possibility of impossibility," as Heidegger thought, or, on the contrary, the "impossibility of all possibility?"

E.L.: It's a possibility in which it is possible to negate the future. Does the relationship between death and time come from the fact that being is finitude? You know that I go a little further than that. I claim in a sense that death is always in a way a murder. Every time someone dies, the whole of humanity is responsible—"in a way" at least. In the sadness caused by someone's death there's something like a feeling of responsibility for this life that has come to an end and in that sense a feeling similar to guilt, as if we were guilty for surviving, as if there were guilt in innocence. In the compassion or participation in mourning, there's maybe an element of guilt before the phenomenon of death.

It's not "seemly" to consider someone's death as if "it didn't concern us," in other words, as if my innocence were absolutely excluded. Of course one can say that it's the finitude of being that implies death, or the original sin I had no part in, and that this is the case whatever the philosophical or theological justification for death. But when you say that death is scandalous, it means that the "survivor" cannot simply and purely wash his hands of the affair. Humanity shares a part of all that's bad in the world.

Q.: In what way is your relationship to time more Bergsonian than Heideggerian? You take up Bergson's sublime idea somewhere that love is the temporality of time.

E.L.: Time is what cannot be foreseen. But it's also promise and surprise and in this sense, love. Bergson doesn't say it like this, but time is an opening, a form of creation despite the mechanized time of machines and clocks.

It's an idea that can be rethought in different ways in human existence. Until Bergson came along, time was what comes to pass, the perishable. Time was impoverished, it was the eternal that counted. The eternal is essentially duration, unicity as such. Bergson is the first to have made of time the purity of the real. For us, time is the purity of real-life experience in Bergsonian duration. The word "purity," *rein* in German, also exists in Heidegger. But it's more limited and purer in Bergson.

Time in Bergson is the real that has lost its perishable character and become spirit. When all is said and done, temporality is the love of the other. Bergsonian duration is the dimension in which the approach of the other can be found. Theology is the basis of duration. The opposite is true in Heidegger, where all human authority and all authenticity are included in his grasping of Being. This is the big difference, roughly speaking, between Bergson's biblical Western spiritualism and Heidegger's pagan, or more precisely, Greek thought.

There was no definition of the spirit of duration in *Sein und Zeit* [*Being and Time*]. The thematics of time carried in itself the malediction of eternity.

Today we have forgotten the reading of *Matter and Memory* and the *Immediate Data of Consciousness,* but we owe to Bergson this sign of purity in the idea of authenticity as duration. There's more hope in Bergson than in Heidegger.

Q.: I remember a lecture you gave in which you spoke superbly of the relationship between the feminine and temporality. You already noted in *Time and the Other* the exceptional place of Eros among human relations and you wrote, "It is a relationship with alterity, with mystery—that is to say, with the future, with what (in a world where there is everything) is never there, with what cannot be there when everything is there" (*TO* 88).

E.L.: Indeed, I think that there's a promise of the future in the feminine. The feminine in the human is like the ecstasy of the future. You've just recalled my paper on Eros in *Time and the Other* where the thematics of the caress as waiting for the pure future was already present.

I've just touched on the problem of feelings, which opens up a lot of dimensions. I asked myself, for example, if gratuitousness and self-interest constitute the ultimate distinction in moral reflection. Does the debate on the reciprocity of feelings sufficiently take these dimensions into account by inquiring about the problem of the nature of generous conduct? The person we are good to is happy, like the person who did some good is happy, but is his happiness not of another order? It's an *otherwise* that would require an indepth analysis, one too long to develop here. The goodness in the act of doing good at least acknowledges differences in nobility and height, which cannot be measured by what is equal and unequal. It's not certain that despite everything that was comparable in the two movements of one for the other, God was thought of in the same way.

Q.: We have a passage in the Talmud [Baba Metzia 62a] in which Rabbi Akiba is discussing with Ben Patura whether a man in the desert has the right to share his water with his companion, knowing that there's not enough for two. Ben Patura says that he should share it, but Rabbi Akiba disagrees: "*Hayekha kodmim,* thy life takes precedence!" Which means that our life is not ours and that God alone can do with it what he will.

E.L.: This is added wisdom, but how it will be judged in heaven, we have no idea. Rabbi Akiba is very concerned about not getting carried away with the "romanticism of suffering." Indeed, this poses the whole problem of the limits of sacrifice. Our life is not ours, to the extent that we have to respect it.

There's another text by Rabbi Akiba which I often quote and which is particularly profound. "Must one look or not at the face of the defendant?" One talmudic doctor replies that one can look at the face even before the verdict has been pronounced. So Rabbi Akiba says, "Before the verdict, one does not look at the face, but after the sentence has been pronounced, one must look."[4] What does this mean? That the sentence given is not irrevocable, a judicial mistake is always possible, that it can be reviewed. I quote this passage to help understand the moment when the prophet suddenly cries out that God will punish the children of Israel for their wrongdoings. Rabbi Akiba teaches us here that it is possible to review the sentence.

In a just state, when a sentence is pronounced, the possibility exists, if one has good cause, to appeal. It's

---

4. [Levinas appears to be referring to a talmudic apologue in Tractate Rosh Hashanah 17b–18a, which he does indeed quote elsewhere, but here Levinas has totally changed his commentary as well as what Rabbi Akiba actually says; see *EN* 230 (reproduced in *IRB* 207), for Levinas's more faithful interpretation of Rabbi Akiba's resolution of the biblical contradiction between Deuteronomy 10:17 and Numbers 6:26.—Trans.]

the same meaning here. Does democracy not consist in reflecting on the authority of power? Even the judiciary?

Q.: What does the Warsaw Ghetto uprising call to mind for you?

E.L.: The uprising is an extraordinary reawakening that put an end to a lot of East European Jewry's assimilation. It wasn't a senseless idea, but a goal for the Jewish existence under threat. It was a truly courageous act given that there mustn't have been much hope. "We can't take it anymore."
I know what life was like at the time in the countries in the East. The uprising was a terrible, inimitable reaction.

Q.: I believe it was the first organized rebellion against the Nazi plan to annihilate the Jews.

E.L.: There was never any acceptance of the Nazi plan, as you can well imagine, but this was the first attempt at self-sacrifice and to sacrifice oneself *for* something.
This is what I see in the despair...like a desperate sacrifice. It's not an event that can be interpreted in any banal way, in just any way at all. Which is why all we can do is to bow down before those who instigated it.

Q.: Do you think that the Polish people are still anti-Semitic, 50 years after the disappearance of Jews from Poland?

E.L.: I don't know, after all, the pope is Polish,[5] and I'm very sensitive to the fact that he asked the nuns in

---

5. [Levinas is referring, of course, to Pope John Paul II, born Karol Wojtyla, who was pope from 1978 until his death in 2005.—Trans.]

the former Auschwitz complex to leave. He wrote to them personally. One can't be insensitive to that. Before, I used to take part regularly in the philosophical meetings at Castel Gandolfo, the pope's summer residence, and I had stopped going the year the Carmelite convent was installed.

Q.: After the Shoah, it seems we can no longer pronounce the terms *hanora* (awesome) and *hagibor* (mighty) in the *Tefillah* (daily prayer), terms used to qualify the Holy One, blessed be He. In the Talmud, in Tractate Yoma [69b], our masters relate that after the desecration of the First Temple, Jeremiah omitted the word *hanora*, and that later Daniel cried out, "Aliens are enslaving His sons. Where are His mighty deeds?" He too omitted the word *hagibor*, "mighty."

E.L.: That's the very topicality of the ambiguity.

Q.: That's not all.

E.L.: No, that's not all. In the complete text from the Midrash, a page falls from heaven, and on the page is written a single word: Truth. The truth of Daniel and Jeremiah is as true as their refutation.

The Great Assembly continues by asserting that the supreme, most fearful type of strength is forbearance. There's no dogmatic solution.

God has several ways to come to the spirit.

Q.: Let's come back to philosophy. For you, ethics always defines man's relationship with his fellow, whereas for Professor Yeshayahu Leibowitz, ethics concerns above all man's relationships toward God, before being concerned with man's relationships toward his fellow.

E.L.: Is he right to separate the two things? Because isn't man's relation to man already in itself what is essential in man's relation to the Eternal? This is not at all a verbal reduction of one to the other. The discovery of the other man's face in the responsibility toward him is how we hear God's voice. One of my books on religious philosophy is entitled *Of God Who Comes to Mind*. God's coming to mind is certainly contemporaneous with the responsibility assumed toward the other's face.

Q.: Is transcendence inseparable from immanence?

E.L.: Absolutely. It's not any easier. It's just as much an occasion for sacrifice. It's no laughing matter.

Q.: When it comes to speaking to Christians, you readily say that for you the incarnation is to be understood literally as the presence of God in the face of the other...

E.L.: I use the expression "in the guise" of the other, but I don't say that the other is the incarnation of God. In any case, there's a relation between the affirmation of God and my relationship toward humanity and the other. This is a logical, paradoxical moment. You encounter God intimately through the other. There's no greater intimacy.

Q.: For the religious Jew, the *mitzvah* [commandment] is also the particular intimacy he has with God. This is what the Christian doesn't understand. You yourself wrote in your preface to Moses Mendelssohn's *Jerusalem* that "the practice of that law, like the study of it, is not the simple expression of faith, but the ultimate intimacy with a God who revealed himself in history" (*ITN* 142).

E.L.: Whatever the intermediaries, the relation to the law is the relation to the other, even in things where it's not evident, such as *kashrut* (Jewish dietary laws), for instance. That's what talmudic thought is all about.

I want to insist on the fact that seeing the face is not like perceiving something. It's very important to grasp this. It's not like seeing a thing, seeing a painting, not at all. It's an immediate relation of responsibility and consequently the word of God. Indeed, there's quite a difference here with Aristotelian logic. There are three of us when there are two of us. What I'm saying shouldn't be understood in terms of substance but in terms of classical philosophy. This third place is unique. God is present. We're already responding to him.

I'm not saying I'm against logic, but these are small repercussions that aren't mathematical, and they imply the presence of human collectivity.

Q.: Isn't your philosophy of substitution, of the responsibility that makes me an irreplaceable being, similar at one point to the ultimate meaning of being conscious of "the unjustified privilege of having survived six million dead"?

E.L.: I don't have the key to this event, but the very principle of man's understanding seems to me to be the responsibility toward the third as humanity's emotion as such. This is where the divine is divine. Its existence stands out from the existence of a chair. This has to be said in an absolutely vigorous manner, not piously.

Q.: This is what you mean when you write precisely in *Of God Who Comes to Mind:* "My deepest thought, which carries all thought, my thought of the infinite, older than the thought of the finite, is the very diachrony of time..., a way of 'being dedicated' before any act of consciousness, and more deeply so than in consciousness, by way of the gratuity of time (in which philosophers managed to fear a vanity or privation)" (*GCM* xiv).

E.L.: Absolutely, but here I'm bringing the idea back to fundamental philosophical categories. In one way or another, this is how European man, and man as such, feel things. To break with these categories is to break with the human message itself.

In this context, welcoming the face prolongs the respect for the other which is God's.

Q.: There's an extraordinary passage in the Torah where it says that God speaks between Moses and Aaron when they're in the Tent of Meeting.
E.L.: It's the third party that's present. Only this shouldn't be said as something pious. It's the initial "You" when addressing someone. It can take other forms, of course.
But I absolutely believe that a society in which there is equality is a society in which there is God. Certain biblical verses have to be read in this way.
Q.: You once wrote, "Jewish man without a *mitzvah* is a danger to the world." What do you mean by this?
E.L.: It means that peace has been broken. You have to link it to what I was saying just now, that the relation to the law is the relation to the other.
The paradox of the expression that "there are three of us when there are two of us" has to be preserved in its very opposition to good sense.
Q.: There is a writer who has been present in your work ever since your first books, even if he seldom appears. I'm speaking of Proust, whereas Kafka is practically absent.
E.L.: You can't ignore Kafka! But the subjectivity in Proust is irreplaceable. The fault is always mine. There's a kind of sadness in Proustian subjectivity. Proust's not one to laugh at his humanity. What's extraordinary in his work is a certain way of being exposed, I'd say a kind of nakedness. Still, this way of being exposed doesn't always take on the form of a *mea culpa*. The Proustian narrative takes place in a climate that's not miserable but exposed. I'm guilty for being guilty.
I would add that all his characters, particularly Albertine, feel guilty, with all the other feelings that emerge without being named, such as shame, cold,

nakedness, loneliness, and despite everything they're already capable of listening to God.

Q.: Are we not witnessing at the close of this century a phenomenon whereby states feel increasingly responsible for the dramas and tragedies that occur throughout the world, such as the breakup of Yugoslavia? Israelis here demonstrate a sense of ethics that cannot but be lauded.

E.L.: And many Christians too, many human beings. It's a nightmare that weighs on us, as if we were responsible. *We* is me. In these contradictory situations, we are guilty for being guilty.

The central idea of my argument is that the other's alterity is my responsibility for him, which is heavy and evasive. The sign of being human is caring for the other—*die Sorge,* as Heidegger says. Caring for the other isn't always something we can see. It's not because we talk about being selfless and altruistic that we have understood humanity, the other. If you think about it, it's an enormous thing, responsibility, when you've done nothing.

Q.: We might come full circle and conclude by linking the extreme urgency that can be found in this *Sorge* with the central idea from the beginning of our dialogue, the hostage. Is the hostage, then, the person who carries the sign of the human in his heart?

E.L.: To be responsible for the other is to be a hostage. This is unfairly so, but this *unfairly* is an essential element of the responsibility. Not paying attention to what goes beyond my own fault, where other people's fault is clearer than what I'm accountable for, this is the constant attitude that moral life entails. Which is why there are contradictions in the definition of responsibility that aren't raised, that are paradoxical to coexistence.

The hostage is the person who works in your place, and if he doesn't work, he is killed. There exists an element of the permanent hostage in society. We are always someone else's hostage, but not so that we can go and complain about it.

Q.: In order, finally, to open up our encounter rather than to bring it to a close, I will ask you if there was any mentor in your youth who left a particular impression on you.

E.L.: A few months ago I was asked to write a personal tribute for one of my mentors. In this short text, which I called *Mitgenommen,* I reminisced about Dr. Moshe Schwabe, who taught me German in Lithuania. I'll read it to you:

> I was born into a Jewish family where the children were spoken to in Russian, in other words where Russian civilization and literature were held in great esteem. But the outbreak of war in 1914 had driven my parents from this progressively Western corner, until after a few stops en route they eventually found themselves in Karkov in the Ukraine, which is where the state school from the town where I was born had been evacuated to. I started attending the school in the autumn of 1916, quite a success for a Jew under the tzarist regime.
>
> Then came the revolution, Communism, and the chaos of civil wars. In 1920, my parents took advantage of a chance to return to Lithuania which had become an independent republic the year previously. It was here, in the last year of a Jewish Russian language High School, that I prepared the leaving certificate, the equivalent of the baccalaureate. My German teacher for this last year was a Jew who was deeply assimilated to Germanic culture, Dr. Moshe Schwabe. He had discovered East European Jewry at the time of the German occupation. He was touched by it and decided to devote himself to it. So he accepted a teaching post in a Jewish high school in Lithuania. But it was the West, and the West as seen through German culture, and German

culture through Goethe, that dazzled us. The hours we spent in class reading *Hermann and Dorothea,* a book that evokes in particular a European dialogue experienced in peacetime, were a preparation for and a promise of the discovery of the pages of *Faust* which, he would say, "are to be read with forty degrees of fever," a promise that kept the best of us in suspense.... But we were spared the fever by the master's wisdom and the year ended with *Poetry and Truth* in which Goethe relates his childhood in Frankfurt and lists the paintings by often obscure painters which embellished the apartment. The obscurity of glory that shocked the young pupils: "Why are they not known?" we would ask. And the master's eminent reply: "Goethe took them with him—*mitgenommen*—into immortality."

And what of Montaigne, Descartes, Pascal, Bergson, these passers-by who take so many people, things, fertile ideas with them into immortality, and by so doing confer dignity upon them... Is that what the West is? Pushkin, Petrarch, Dante, Shakespeare... Looks that embellish the world.

Moshe Schwabe's West was realized in 1951 in Jerusalem, where he was a teacher of Greek.[6]

---

6. Levinas, "Mitgenommen," 227–28.

PART TWO

*From the Phenomenology
of the Face
to a Philosophy
of the Breach*

1

From the Epiphany of the Face to the Idea of Holiness

WHAT CAN BE DONE TO OPPOSE HUMAN FOLLY? Answers to this question have not come from the most famous philosophers but from men and women often unknown in their lifetime but whose work was revealed in all its importance once they had departed this earthly life. It may be that Emmanuel Levinas belongs to this family of thinkers, alongside people such as Simone Weil and Franz Rosenzweig, whose fame was greater still after his death.

First of all, by recalling that Levinas belongs to the great Western philosophical tradition from Plato to Bergson, Husserl and Heidegger, one can measure the incommensurable breach effected in his work, and above all during the last 20 years, by the fundamental notion of holiness.

In his *Talmudic Readings* he had already noted the primacy of the holy over the sacred.[1]

In a certain sense, it is with the intrusion of the holy and holiness into his discourse that the considerable originality of his thought and work is brought in a way to completion. Not content with having reintroduced God into philosophical discourse—but a God a thousand miles from Descartes' or Pascal's—Levinas comes and posits humanity's holiness as the only way to answer our initial question: what can be done to oppose "the world's tragic folly," which occupied so much of Michel Foucault's thought? One further word before we get into our subject, on this God who in Levinas comes to mind. In my opinion he bears some relation to the Way, the *Dao* in Chinese thought—that of Laozi and Confucius (Master Kong)—according to which the idea of God merges with heaven (*tian*) and which in Confucius's *Analects* becomes the permanent referent for the ethics presiding over the relations between beings.

So let us walk along the Way Levinas's thought opens up for us, follow this philosopher whose language bears the inflections of Péguy.

It is around what is concrete in the epiphany of the face as that which gives meaning to all human life that I will ask the question of the meaning of Being in Levinas's philosophy.

---

1. [Levinas published four volumes of talmudic readings in his lifetime; a fifth was published posthumously. In English, they are published under the following titles: *Nine Talmudic Readings, Beyond the Verse, In the Time of the Nations,* and *New Talmudic Readings*. *Difficult Freedom* also contains a number of talmudic readings on the subject of messianism.—Trans.]

A few years ago a French weekly devoted its front page to Sartre with the headline: "Sartre, the passion of error."[2] For Levinas, it would be more apt to say: Levinas or the passion of the other, in the two senses of the word "passion." So let us ask the question of Being, which is the founding principle of all possibility of an *otherwise than being,* which Levinas never had coincide with a "being otherwise," as if *otherwise* could not be satisfied with its place as an adverb affixed to being in a secondary position as regards the fact of being, but rather that it determined in its precellence its very precedence over the verb *to be* at its foundation.

Let us go back to the first lines of Levinas's major work *Otherwise Than Being or Beyond Essence:* "If transcendence has meaning, it can only signify the fact that the *event of being,* the *esse,* the *essence,* passes over to what is other than being.... Transcendence is passing over to being's *other,* otherwise than being. Not *to be otherwise,* but *otherwise than being.* And not to not-be; passing over is not here equivalent to dying" (*OB* 3).

These first lines by way of expounding on the problematic give us three fundamental words: transcendence, meaning, and the *event of being.* We should ask ourselves at this point whether we should not read this opening in parallel or together with the deeply moving exordium that opens the book, transmitting its secret core, so unspeakable that Levinas prefers to resort to the Hebrew for his second epigraph naming his murdered parents. Here then are the very first lines: "To the memory of those who

---

2. [Saint Cheron is referring to *Le Point,* dated January 15, 2000.—Trans.]

were closest among the six million assassinated by the National Socialists, and of the millions on millions of all confessions and all nations, victims of the same hatred of the other man, the same anti-semitism" (*OB* v).

The entire philosophy of *Otherwise Than Being or Beyond Essence* begins here. How to philosophize from out of this gaping hole, this abyss that left Martin Heidegger cold? Does this "otherwise than being" refer in truth to an otherwise than dying, the very dying that is in question in the preliminary lines of the epigraph? In other words, what relation can be discerned between these two modalities of being and dying? Otherwise than being does not signify, then, *being otherwise*. On the other hand, is there a dying and an *otherwise than dying* whose memory might make us seek to attain an *otherwise than being*?

I would like to show how Levinas starts with the epiphany of the face and ends up with a transcendence that can no longer be defined in relation to God but in relation to forgiveness and responsibility, and further still to the love that passes from one being to another.

Otherwise than being would in a way be the opposite of being otherwise, which is still a *conatus essendi,* a being persevering in its being, the "detestable self" referred to by Pascal. But then would otherwise than being not be a second fundamental alterity? Let us suppose that otherwise than being is a sublimated egoism. In *Gorgias*, Plato writes that we are not afraid of death but of "the idea of not having been just."[3] At the same time, in China, the philosopher Mencius taught that "For every man there are things he cannot bear to happen to others."[4] The other

---

3. See Plato, *Gorgias*.
4. See Mencius, *Mencius*.

name of otherwise than being is benevolence, or the infinite, or the Good.

How then in Levinas does the notion of meaning develop out of the notion of being, given his double-rootedness, the philosophical and phenomenological on the one hand, and the biblical and talmudic on the other? At a time when existentialism and structuralism, the Lacanian school and political philosophy, were all indisputably preeminent, Levinas in France, with Ricoeur, Jankélévitch and a few others, notably Lyotard and Derrida, was a philosopher in the margins of the great contemporary trends of the renewal of meaning. Not that Levinas passed through Derridean deconstruction—"thought of the origin and of the limits of the question *'what is...?,'* the question that dominates the whole of the history of philosophy"[5]—rather, Levinas deconstructed ontology as a fundamental notion.

Has philosophy forgotten Being and lost the meaning of ontology, as Heidegger believed, or has it forgotten, rather, the Good, as Levinas believed?[6] Levinas wanted to add an otherwise than thinking to the otherwise than being, beginning by questioning the foundations of Western philosophy after the collapse of moral and philosophical values with the advent of Nazism and the implementation of the Shoah, not forgetting, during the same period, Stalinism. For in order to think the holiness of being as being more fundamental than ontology, was it not in all evidence necessary to found an otherwise than thinking?

---

5. Derrida, "Entretien inédit avec Roger-Pol Droit."
6. See André de Muralt's preface to Tornay, *L'Oubli du bien*.

What part did Heidegger have in this collapse, from *Sein und Zeit* through to his rectorate speech in 1933, demonstrating that too much being could end up slipping into fascist politics, because being is sometimes accompanied by the forgetting of the other's fundamental alterity. In his *Histoire de la pensée* [*History of Thought*], Jean-Louis Dumas writes, "it is not man but being that is at the center of Heidegger's austere thinking: it is not an anthropology, which would bring us back to Feuerbach, but a fundamental ontology. The authentic behavior of being-there is 'freedom for death.'"[7] The renewal of meaning in Levinas takes off with *Totality and Infinity* and ends with the masterly *Otherwise Than Being,* which itself would open up a final field of research concerning the moment the word God begins to signify.

To philosophically renew God's advent to the mind, following from Descartes and Pascal, but from Kierkegaard too, this is the great speculative enterprise of the thinker who introduced Husserl and Heidegger into the country of Bergson, a philosopher the author of *Sein und Zeit* claimed not to have read.

Let us deepen our approach, by way of *Totality and Infinity,* to the change that takes place in Levinas when he resorts to the highly charged word "epiphany," a word that takes on here the value of an inception and which Levinas prefers to the word "manifestation," which had already appeared in *Discovering Existence with Husserl.*[8] Epiphany with a tripartite signification—theological,

---

7. Dumas, *Histoire de la pensée,* 275.
8. [*Discovering Existence with Husserl* is a truncated version of the title of Levinas's first collection of essays, *En découvrant l'existence chez Husserl et Heidegger,* from which five chapters are taken and to which Saint Cheron is referring.—Trans.]

poetic, and philosophical—clear to all of us and which also explains the great interest Levinas devotes to it. "The epiphany of the face qua face opens humanity... in the eyes that look at me" (*TI* 213).

In *Otherwise Than Being or Beyond Essence* the word has acquired its intrinsic power, its completeness, corresponding to its passage to a superior level of ethics, wholly consistent with the movement from the being of *Dasein* to the "otherwise than being." This passage from immanence to transcendence, from ontology to ethics, can pride itself on being one of the Ways toward holiness, which itself is a superior form of responsibility that goes so far as to become the substitution for the other, to become "the taking upon oneself of the ultimate gift of dying for another" (*GCM* 163), as Levinas puts it in the final pages of *Of God Who Comes to Mind*. Only heroes, martyrs, or saints can achieve this form of transcendence of being for which the other is the person for whom I can sacrifice myself, offer myself. "The transcendence of the revelation lies in the fact that the 'epiphany' comes in the saying of him that received it" (*OB* 149).

Epiphany is more than an apparition, it is like a Revelation, in that it "reveals" the infinite.

With the "epiphany of the face," it is no longer a question of the face in its plastic form according to the criteria of beauty or ugliness, young or old, but the face beyond its deceptive, essentially ephemeral appearance, the face in its unique dimension as a human countenance. The human countenance is above all an evocation, a reminder of suffering and death. The human face carries within it the trace and the reflection of humanity, as well as the inexorable reminder of weakness and misfortune.

In the recent memory of the genocides perpetrated against various peoples, every name, every victim's face, torn from oblivion, represent dozens, indeed hundreds of thousands of others who disappeared, many without so much as a trace. It is in this sense too that every human face bears the presence of the world. I would like, then, to reflect upon the notion of meaning. To begin to speak, to begin to philosophize, is to pose one single question before any other. I quote here a little known text by Levinas, one that deserves attention. It is entitled "Amour et révélation" ["Love and revelation"]: "I believe there exists a question par excellence, a question whose content determines the form of the question: the question of death. A question par excellence in the uprightness of the face but a question too in which I am being asked for; the face is the fact that I am being asked for, summoned."[9] This is the first question, and the first exposition of the question of being in Levinas; initially, it is a response to the fundamental questioning that humanity is faced with in its ability to transcend its own mortality.

In Levinasian metaphysics, in the beginning was the face and the face was inseparable from an ethical word. What does this mean, if not that "in the approach of the face, flesh is made word, and the caress a Saying"?[10] No longer *Verbum caro factum est* but *Caro verbum facta est*. This is an extraordinary philosophical break. This is where Levinas resorts to maternity as a superior stage of the human condition. Is there holiness in maternity? The term "holiness," which in philosophical discourse raises the question of an amphibiology, forces us to reflect too on the metaphysical overtones of the term. Why does Levinas, raised in the Jewish tradition, use this term rather than "justice"? Because rather than the Hebrew

---

9. Levinas, "Amour et révélation," 142.
10. Ibid., 150.

word *tzadik* (just) or *tzedakah* (justice), Levinas prefers the term *kadosh*, holy, or *kedusha*, holiness, which philosophically and theologically is a higher stage of justice. Holiness is what is above justice, the holy person is superior to the just person who, as the meaning suggests, is simply just. Now, our tradition also has its martyrs and saints, even if it prefers to use, in French at least, the word "just" [*juste*], in order to set itself off from Christianity and above all from the Catholic Church.

Woman incarnates the passage from the carnal to the spiritual, from what is not essentially a matter of the flesh. Through the gift of life, by procreation, woman transcends what is principally a matter of desire, the carnal, the erotic, and transforms it into a neverending responsibility, namely to accept life inside her, at the expense of her own freedom, of her own well-being. It is by transcending oneself in this way, physically and metaphysically, that Levinas can write, "in the approach of the face, flesh is made word." The feminine occupies an important place in Levinas's philosophical, biblical, and talmudic thought. Woman is the height of the human. Two magnificent passages in *Otherwise Than Being* bear this out: "In maternity what signifies is a responsibility for others, to the point of substitution for others and suffering both from the effect of persecution and from the persecuting itself in which the persecutor sinks. Maternity, which is bearing par excellence, bears even responsibility for the persecuting by the persecutor" (*OB* 75). And "Maternity in the complete being 'for the other' which characterizes it, which is the very signifyingness of signification, is the ultimate sense of this vulnerability" (*OB* 108).

It is with this paroxysmic dimension of responsibility for the other—too Christian for some, but for Levinas "the essential, primary and fundamental structure of subjectivity," that *Otherwise Than Being* goes beyond *Totality and Infinity.* For Paul Ricoeur, this notion of responsibility going so far as to be the condition or uncondition of the hostage represents the excessive, hyperbolic character of Levinas's thought. He is right, but this does not mean there is not a rare dimension of philosophy mixed with holiness in this desire to bring about, in a totally immoderate way, substitutive, sacrificial, oblatory love, beyond any Christian design. Is there not here a way of redeeming the moral debt of philosophers who from Plato to Heidegger have made a pact with tyrants in the name of this "Western logic [which] is tyrannical 'by definition'"?[11]

Only mothers and a few saints—or the just—pass to "the other of being" in this way. Chinese philosophy, which Levinas knew little about, has a concept from Confucius onwards of the Sovereign Good called the *Ren.* It is a compound of the element of man and the number 2, in other words, alterity in its pure state. In the *Analects* (VI, 28) Confucius writes, "Seek within yourself the idea of what you can do for others—this will put you on the path of *ren.*"[12] Anne Cheng reminds us that this virtue of humanity is so rare "that Confucius judges nobody worthy of the qualification."[13]

To philosophically renew God's advent to the mind, following from Descartes and Pascal, but from Kierkegaard too, this is what Levinas was finally working on during the last 15 years of his life: from an *otherwise than being* to an *otherwise than thinking,* beginning by calling into question the very foundations of Western philosophy.

---

11. Arendt, *Journal de pensée,* 1:60.
12. See Confucius, *The Analects.*
13. Cheng, in Confucius, *Entretiens avec Confucius,* 20.

Is this "otherwise than thinking" not the same as a "beyond the coming of God to the mind," just as Plato in the *Republic* speaks of a "beyond essence"? This philosophy contains such a profoundly new meaning, taking the form of a beyond ontology and a different path to phenomenology—even if Levinas remains a phenomenologist—that one cannot not qualify it as a metaphysics, or better yet as a *meta*ethics. Even if ethics is no more a "first philosophy" than ontology, as Jacques Rolland puts it in his remarkable philosophical essay *Parcours de l'autrement: Lecture d'Emmanuel Levinas* [*Pathways of the Otherwise: A Reading of Emmanuel Levinas*].[14] But Blanchot notes precisely in Levinas's thought "a philosophical upheaval that puts ethics at the beginning."[15]

Nothing would be further from the truth than to confuse the ethics of the author of *Totality and Infinity* with morality and its halo of laws and prohibitions. Likewise, it bears no relation to the *Foundation of the Metaphysics of Morals* in which Kant clearly establishes the primacy of duty toward oneself over the duty toward others. No, it can be defined only as holiness. This is where this philosophy is so courageous, for having taken holiness out of the unique domain of religious transcendence and having introduced it into the domain of reason, of the conceptual and at the same time of metaphysics. But it is just as dangerous not to ask the question of the limits of radical good. As Hannah Arendt asks, how, in the name of this responsibility, does one not go "against the moral law"?[16]

---

14. See Rolland, *Parcours de l'autrement.*
15. Blanchot, "Ce qu'il nous a appris."
16. Arendt, *Journal de pensée,* 1:202.

This desire to introduce holiness into the ranks of philosophical categories is the outcome and completion of the consciousness that dwelt within Levinas for so long. It is a question that has been frequently watered down, criticized even by certain philosophers disdainful of the fields they know nothing about or which they relegate to the margins of philosophy—not to mention those who under the cloak of criticism still show an anti-Semitic allegiance when they call a philosopher of Jewish origin or affiliation a nonphilosopher.

As for those of us who wonder what philosophy still has to teach us, it is our duty to take heed both of the philosophy that considers itself the wisdom of love and of this love as an otherwise than loving.

2

Sartre and Levinas: Is There a Dialogue?

EXISTENTIALISM... IS ABLE TO OPPOSE anti-Semitism....
The presence of an existentialist humanism, that is to say... of a humanism that would assimilate the fundamental experiences of the modern world—this is Sartre's essential contribution to our cause, the cause of humanity."[1] These lines written by Emmanuel Levinas in June 1947, shortly after a lecture by Jean-Paul Sartre, sponsored by the Alliance Israélite Universelle in Paris and delivered in its Salle de la Chimie, are the first by the philosopher of *Totality and Infinity* on his already illustrious contemporary.

The first meeting between the two men, the two philosophers, took place just after *Nausea* came out in 1938, at the house of their elder Gabriel Marcel, in other words, several years before the publication of *Being and*

---

1. Levinas, "Existentialism and Anti-Semitism," 28, 31.

Nothingness in 1943, smack in the middle of the catastrophe. For Sartre, Levinas's name had appeared in 1930, the year of the publication of *The Theory of Intuition in Husserl's Phenomenology*. After having thumbed through the volume, Sartre apparently declared, "All this I wanted to say myself, but Husserl has already said it" (*IRB* 43).

HUSSERL AND NOT LEVINAS

Nausea was the first book in which Levinas discovered Sartre's thought, a discovery that would long remain a distant admiration and, moreover, one-sided—up until the turning point of the last ten years of Sartre's life in the 1970s. Yet in 1964 Levinas wrote a letter to the laureate of the Nobel Prize for Literature (there is no Nobel Prize for Philosophy), congratulating him for refusing the prize. The mentor of a whole generation never replied. In his missive, which the author qualified as "important," Levinas wrote that for having refused the Nobel Prize, Sartre "perhaps was the only man who had the right to speak, and maybe this was the moment where he had to speak: to go to Nasser in Egypt to propose peace with Israel. Crazy idea! But I told him, 'You're the only man Nasser will listen to'" (*IRB* 43).

When Levinas recalled this episode, how could he not have felt offended? This was an offense about which he could not keep silent and which he reveals at the end of his anecdote. "I was told that, receiving this letter, he asked, 'Who is this Levinas anyway?' Had he forgotten? Had he forgotten *The Theory of Intuition in Husserl's Phenomenology?*" asks Levinas in conclusion (*IRB* 43). The offense, it seems, dissipated when Sartre invited Levinas to his home to ask him to contribute to the special issue of *Les temps modernes* he was preparing on the Palestinian question. Levinas wrote a text for the illustrious review, which he entitled "Politics After!" on the historic meeting between Sadat and Begin and the hope for peace that had been born.[2]

THE OTHER IN THE DIALOGUE WITH SARTRE

As we reach this unique philosophical moment from which, on the one hand, the "epiphany of the face" is opened to holiness and, on the other, transcendence is understood without the assistance of religion, we might make a side move to Sartre, to *Humanism and the Other* in which Levinas, in a superb development concerning the trace, writes these lines: "And Sartre, though stopping short of a full analysis, makes the striking observation that the Other is a pure hole in the world. The Other proceeds from the *absolutely Absent*" (*HO* 39).

In his lectures from 1947 to 1948, published in 1983 under the title *Time and the Other,* Levinas was already questioning Sartrean existentialism: "In Sartre's philosophy there is some sort of angelical present. The whole weight of existence being thrown back onto the past, the freedom of the present is already situated above matter" (*TO* 62).

Levinas wants to find the freedom of the present, dispossessed of all its weighty matter. Hence the "angelical present" can be understood not as a quality or an appreciation but, on the contrary, as a criticism of Sartrean naiveté—"which is also the naiveté of all ontology, no matter how critical it claims to be,"[3] and which makes of the present of consciousness the point of departure for his reflection. In place of this naiveté Levinas will substitute

---

2. [See *BV* 188–95; reprinted edition, 182–88.—Trans.]
3. Tornay, *L'oubli du bien,* 123.

the true metaphysics that for him is ethics. And yet when Sartre writes that the *cogito* cannot be the origin of philosophy, has he not reached a spectacular problematic? In *Being and Nothingness* Sartre asserts that the question of the other "should not be posited in terms of the *cogito;* on the contrary, the existence of the Other renders the *cogito* possible as the abstract moment when the self is apprehended as an object."[4] Insofar as it is the ego's consciousness, itself rendered possible by the appearance of the other and whose measure gives meaning to everything, the Sartrean *cogito* creates a deceptive tangent to Levinas's ethics.

Without needing to go further into these prolegomena, it is easy to understand that Levinas has a radically different conception of the *cogito* and consequently of the other. In the final pages of *Totality and Infinity,* the philosopher comes back to Sartre with the intention of criticizing the relation between the Sartrean conception of the other and freedom:

> The encounter with the Other in Sartre threatens my freedom, and is equivalent to the fall of my freedom under the gaze of another freedom. Here perhaps is manifested most forcefully being's incompatibility with what remains veritably exterior. But to us here there rather appears the problem of the justification of freedom: does not the presence of the Other put in question the naïve legitimacy of freedom? Does not freedom appear to itself as a shame for itself? And, reduced to itself, as a usurpation? (*TI* 303)

The last instance of freedom, curiously, is the appearance of the other, both in Levinas and in Sartre, but for inversely proportional reasons. If, for Levinas, my

---

4. Sartre, *Being and Nothingness,* 236.

freedom, in what is fundamental to it, begins with my obligation to the Other, coming before being requested, before being called for, for Sartre it seems to end with it.

THE IRRUPTION OF KAFKA AND TRANSCENDENCE

Few critics have stopped to ponder the fact that between Sartre and Levinas lies the emblematic work of Kafka. Kafka is closer to Sartre than to Levinas, but for both philosophers his meaning is inseparable from a certain metaphysical anguish, inherent in both the Jewish and the human souls. We might almost say that what our two philosophers have in common with Kafka is that neither has anything to say about him—or almost nothing, to be precise. This is not a question of distance but on the contrary because of a quasi-unsayable proximity, because Kafka's work exceeds meaning and consequently exceeds all philosophy. In his essay on Blanchot's novel *Aminadab,* Sartre opposes Blanchot's discourse on Kafka and writes:

> About Kafka I have nothing more to say, except that he is one of the greatest and most unique writers of our time. And besides, he was the first on the scene; the technique he chose corresponded in him to a need. If he shows us human life everlastingly troubled by an impossible transcendence, it is because he believes in the existence of this transcendence. Only, it is beyond our reach. His universe is both fantastic and rigorously true.[5]

Saying so much with so few words, these lines cannot fail to remind us of the only note written by Levinas on the tragic visionary from Prague, in the final pages of his

---

5. Sartre, "*Aminadab,* or the Fantastic," 69.

book *Of God Who Comes to Mind*—not in the body of the text but, to be precise, an endnote, right at the very end, but one of major significance:

> Here, in the guise of a biblical fable, I will recall the books that seem to constitute the "bible" of the contemporary literary world: Kafka's works. Beyond the labyrinths and the blind alleys of the Power, the Hierarchy, and the Administration which mislead and separate men, there rises in Kafka's work the problem of human identity, itself placed in question under the accusation, without culpability, of its right to be and that of the innocence of the very coming to pass of the adventure of being. (*GCM* 209–10)

How is it possible not to see in these two remarks a decisive, metaphysical connection between Levinas and Sartre concerning this unspeakable transcendence and this "accusation without culpability"—burning, incandescent, visible on every line, in every word—which converge toward the waiting for a deliverance that itself cannot speak its name? Then again, in an interview from 1980, the author of *Otherwise Than Being or Beyond Essence* was to return to Kafka one more time:

> Further, think of Kafka. He describes a culpability without crime, a world in which man never gets to know the accusations charged against him. We see there the genesis of the problem of meaning. It is not only the question "Is my life righteous?" but rather, "Is it righteous to be?" This is very important, for we always measure out the good on the basis of the being that is. (*IRB* 163)

In Levinas, the question "Is it righteous to be?" takes on a dimension that is not just ethical, naturally, but particularly tragic because it necessarily refers back to the question posed, in its most essential intimacy, by "the unjustified privilege of having survived six million deaths" (*PN* 120).

A transcendence beyond reach, as in *The Castle, The Metamorphosis,* and above all in the parable *Before the Law.* Sartre was very stricken by the last lines of this fable. One may even think that he read the man from the country's ultimate question and the doorkeeper's ultimate reply as having particular significance. In truth, Kafka is posing an unfathomable question: "Everyone strives to reach the Law,... so how does it happen that for all these many years no one but myself has ever begged for admittance?" And the doorkeeper delivers his final words like a mortal blow: "No one else could ever be admitted here, since this gate was made only for you. I am now going to shut it."[6]

In *Being and Nothingness,* Sartre comments, "Such is precisely the case with the for-itself if we may add in addition that *each man makes for himself his own gate.*"[7] Yet Sartre's remark cannot of course exhaust the meaning of these final questions. And Sartre is not claiming to do so. But that everyone should be unto himself—in an established and explicit for-self—his own gate, indicates *a contrario* that all ontology condemns itself and that the epiphany of the face alone can break the closure of the for-self which cannot by itself burst into a *Für-Sorge,* a for-the-other. What is this for-the-other precisely? It is a for-self in which anguish for the other comes before the fear for oneself.

---

6. "Before the Law," in Kafka, *Penguin Complete Short Stories,* 4.
7. Sartre, *Being and Nothingness,* 550.

SARTRE AND THE JEWS

We have reached the big question. Sartre and the Jews. This is the reason for our encounter. If Sartre and Levinas, then, in the strictly philosophical domain, diverge significantly without ever really being diametrically opposed to one another, Sartre's final position on Jewish thought, as it appears in *Hope Now,* his last interviews with Benny Lévy, reveals a certain proximity with Levinas as the philosopher and thinker of Jewishness. I would like to quote here an initial important passage from the interviews:

> J-PS: The Jewish religion implies that this world will end and, at the same moment, another world will appear—another world that will be made of this one but in which things will be differently arranged. There is also another theme I like: the Jewish dead—and others too, for that matter—will come back to life, they will return to earth. Contrary to the Christian conception, they—the present Jewish dead—have no existence other than that of the grave, but they will be reborn as living beings in this new world. This new world is the end.
> BL: What interests you about that?
> J-PS: The finality to which every Jew is more or less consciously inclined and which must ultimately reunite humanity. It is this end, which is at bottom social as well as religious and which only the Jewish people...
> ...If you like, it's the beginning of the existence of men who live for each other. In other words, it's an ethical end. Or, more exactly, it is ethics. The Jew thinks that the end of the world, of this world, and the upsurge of the other will result in the appearance of the ethical existence of men who live for one another.[8]

---

8. Sartre and Lévy, *Hope Now,* 105–06.

What follows is equally striking. In response to a remark by Benny Lévy noting that ethics is not the ultimate goal, in other words the final instance of the Jewish conception of the world and its corollary, the messianic era, Sartre, seemingly ignoring his friend's words, keeps going and pursues his train of thought: "The question is to find the ultimate end, the moment when ethics will be simply and truly the way in which human beings live in relation to each other."[9]

These pages are disturbing for more than one of us, and in my turn I ask whether the later Sartre has not become a Levinasian.

In the final analysis Sartre ascribes to the Jews the messianism of which the non-Jewish equivalent, for him, would be revolution. The Jews are the first to have conceived of history as capable of or having to have, rather, a means of escape, an exit provided by a transcendent event and not a banal terrestrial end of the world. There has to be a redemption to correspond to the beginning and it has to be a true deliverance. A deliverance from history, evidently, but also a deliverance out of history. Should Sartre's political and revolutionary struggle be understood by way of these two human categories of the Jew and the non-Jew as a kind of secular messianism? Who would have understood it as such before he explained himself so clearly to Benny Lévy?

We are well aware that we are faced with an extremely serious problem because with Hegel we have a totality of history, and Israel escapes this totality of history, not by some quirk or a unilateral decision by some decision maker, but because of Hegel himself who *a priori*

---

9. Ibid., 106.

excludes the Jewish people from history. This questioning of the meaning of history for the author of *Nausea* was a kind of *Atemwende*, a "breathturn" or "turning of the breath," to borrow Celan's powerful term.[10] At the time of *Anti-Semite and Jew*, when confronted with the question of the possibility of a Jewish history, Sartre replies that there is no Jewish history. What he understood at the time by history was history in the Hegelian sense of the word, in other words, the history of a people on a land with a historical and *de facto* political legitimacy. He had not weighed up the relevance of thinking of the history of a people who had certainly been dispersed and exiled, a people without a land, but one that formed one united people through a reality that was at the very least geopolitical and exilic, and embodying one common destiny.

If there was still no Jewish history for the philosopher of existentialism—and moreover for atheistic existentialism—there was at least an incredibly forceful *Jewish destiny*. Confronted with the messengers of certain essential trends of the Jewish thought that thinks of itself as such, and with his encounters with Claude Lanzmann, Benny Lévy, and his adopted daughter Arlette Elkaïm-Sartre, Jean-Paul Sartre had to come to the logical conclusion that he had been mistaken, which explains what he asserted to Benny Lévy: "The philosophy of history isn't the same if there's a Jewish history or if there isn't. But obviously there is a Jewish history."[11]

And Sartre will follow Benny Lévy's logic right through to the end when he accepts the hypothesis that Hegel

---

10. See Celan, *Breathturn*.
11. Sartre and Lévy, *Hope Now*, 103.

"sought to get rid of the Jew,"[12] whereas it is the Jew precisely who allows us to get away from the concept of history that Hegel wanted to impose on the West, and almost succeeded until Rosenzweig who, with Husserl, was one of the first philosophers, in his masterpiece *Der Stern der Erlösung* [*The Star of Redemption*], to discredit the concept of totality and of the totality of history in particular.

In *Totality and Infinity*, Emmanuel Levinas in his turn marks a break with the Hegelian philosophy of history.

MALRAUX, SARTRE, AND THE JEWS

So what does it actually consist of, this reality of a dispersed people, with no true common history throughout its dispersal since the exile from Judea and the destruction of the temple in Jerusalem in 70 CE? Sartre provides a crucial reply to this question by agreeing with the Jewish conception of history that Levinas had never ceased developing and which, beyond Levinas, was also the view Malraux had of the Jewish people.

We had been in no doubt that Sartre and Malraux would be in agreement on at least one thing: their relation to the Jewish people and to Israel. Hence Sartre's following reply to Benny Lévy:

> All things considered, I believe that for the Jew the essential thing is that for several thousand years he has had a relationship with a single God; he has been a monotheist, and that's what distinguished him from all the other ancient peoples who all had

---

12. Ibid., 104.

many gods, and that's what has made the Jew absolutely essential and autonomous.[13]

I want to come back a moment to Malraux and to what he said about the particular relationship of the Jews to God, in his preface to a volume published in 1955, entitled *Israël*, when the Hebrew State was not yet ten years old:

> Israel was perhaps the only Eastern people to take God seriously....This nation...allied a determined rationalism to their pleas that were thousands of years old...its people laid waste by God and no less so by justice, and not wanting to forget it when it discovered the reason of State....There is no State of Israel without the Bible, without what the Bible becomes in a transformation in which the divine itself has a part.[14]

In the lines we previously quoted Sartre is not talking about the State of Israel but Malraux's comments on the exemplary nature of the Jewish people's relationship to God—the Unique One, *HaShem* as we call him, in other words, the Name—are surprisingly similar in tone to Sartre's. What is less disturbing in Malraux is more so in Sartre, namely, that they both took into account what we will call, as Levinas of course does, "holy history."

THE DIALOGUE WITH BENNY LÉVY

To recall holy history with Levinas is to underline what Sartre calls in the interview with Benny Lévy the "metaphysical character" of the Jew—a metaphysical character that by nature is inseparable from the religious and,

---

13. Ibid., 104.
14. Malraux, "Texte liminaire," 9, 10, 11.

if we may say so, transcendental character linking it to God.

We are well aware of touching here on just how insightful the Sartre-Levinas dialogue is, namely the fundamental critique of Hegel. In one of his three texts devoted to Sartre, Levinas writes, "If there is a Jewish history, Hegel is not true. And there is a Jewish history." And Levinas adds:

> That the history of the Jewish people, in which the hope of the Jewish State on earth has always been essential, could have sown the seed of doubt in Sartre's mind as to the sovereign and majestic architecture of Hegelian logic—what is the meaning of this if not that the State in question does not open onto a purely political history, that which is written by the victors and the proud, but also that such a project, far from signifying any nationalist particularism, is one of the possibilities of the difficult humanity of the human?[15]

This is not just a brilliant exposition in which Jewish destiny becomes in short one of the many paths open to humanity, but an extension of the thought Sartre expressed in his dialogue with Benny Lévy. Did Sartre, like Levinas, understand Jewish destiny as being a universal paradigm?

What a change in thought for the author of *Anti-Semite and Jew* who right after the war disputed the Jew having his own essence! In a text from 1947 entitled "Jewish Being," published in the review *Confluences,* Levinas, who understood that the young Sartre could contest this essence, foresaw in a way 30 years ahead of the time that

---

15. Levinas, "A Language Familiar to Us," 201. [Translation slightly modified.—Trans.]

the later Sartre could profoundly open up to the complexity of Jewish being when he writes:

> Thus, even if it is true that the Jewish fact exists bare, indeterminate in its essence, and called to choose an essence for itself according to the Sartrean framework, this fact is, in its very facticity, inconceivable without election. *The Jewish fact is not like this because he was plumped full of holy history, he refers to holy history because he is a fact like this.* In other words, the Jew is the very entrance of the religious event into the world; better yet, he is the impossibility of a world without religion.[16]

I do not know if Sartre ever read these lines, but after his dialogue with Benny Lévy he would have been the first to express surprise at discovering them, as if he had begun to discover another way of thinking Jewishness and the Jewish fact, inseparable from the very idea of holy history and, as Levinas says here, inseparable from the idea that the Jew bears witness with all his being to the "impossibility of a world without religion."

A world without religion, perhaps, but there is something else to take note of here, because this "impossibility of a world without religion" can be found, fascinatingly, in Hinduism as well as in Judaism. Is Judaism the bearer of something of a quite different nature to this relation in itself essential to a world in which the religious and the holy are in some sense *obligatory*? No, but they are necessary.

In the Jewish condition there is an experience that cannot be surpassed, what we might call, with Levinas, the human *uncondition* as such. And here we would like to return one last time to Levinas's short but major text in

---

16. Levinas, "Being Jewish," 209.

which in a few forceful, highly stylized pages he analyzes the essence of Jewish alterity, inasmuch as, as he says, it is "the fulfillment of the human condition as fact, personhood and freedom."[17]

Here, then, are the lines from 1947, the year following the first publication of *Anti-Semite and Jew:*

> And its entire originality consists in breaking with a world that is without origin and simply present. It is situated from the very start in a dimension that Sartre cannot apprehend. It is not situated there for theological reasons, but for reasons of experience. Its theology explicates its facticity.
>
> Concretely, this dimension is lived by each Jew in his feeling that he exists metaphysically.[18]

Well, it can certainly not be denied that the later Sartre was able not to "apprehend" but to understand metaphysically the Jew's existence.

To conclude this no doubt rather partial approach to the two philosophers, we would like to come back to this new thought and reread the theologico-political reflections Sartre seems to use to reply to the Levinas of 1947, through Benny Lévy, by juxtaposing the Jewish theory of history, "the end of this world," with the resurrection of the dead.

The Jewish conception of the end of times is indeed sometimes likened to a new Creation sustained by a messianic faith announcing the world's salvation brought about by the whole of humanity acknowledging the living God, and by inference acknowledging that the Jews are effectively the messengers of God in the plan of salvation. The time of redemption is inseparable from humanity's social

---

17. Ibid., 210.
18. Ibid., 210.

restoration, or more precisely the world's *shalomization*,[19] a world in which peace and fraternity between human beings would no longer be contradicted with the passing of every moment, every day, every night.

Next to the whole of Israel—for as the Talmud says in the Tractate Sanhedrin (90a): "Kol Yisrael yesh lahem 'helek le'olam haba" [All Israel have a portion in the world to come][20]—stand the Just of the nations, "Tzaddikei oumot ha'olam."

What appeals to Sartre is the idea, on the one hand, that the dead, according to the Jewish conception, have no other destiny than to remain dead while awaiting the final redemption and, on the other, that the heavenly Jerusalem, to use a more Christian than Jewish expression, is embodied in the this-worldly, in the humanity that has been redeemed and atoned for. Not that the messianic era will be played out somewhere in the heavenly expanses, between Earth and Mars! Not at all. But rather in what is earthly and concrete, where the universal *Shalom* will have replaced ignorance and desire, the two seeds of all the hatred in the world, of all the violence in the world.

---

19. [A neologism Saint Cheron forms from the Hebrew word for peace, *shalom*.—Trans.]

20. [The Gemara is quoting the Mishnah Tractate Sanhedrin 10:1.—Trans.]

3

Death and the Other or the Dialogue with Malraux

No RELIGION, WITH THE EXCEPTION perhaps of Buddhism, has ever provided an answer, or is capable of providing an answer, to the two essentially unanswerable questions of *what* and *why* death is. While Christianity and Hinduism have given particular thought to this double question, having death signify above all a passage toward a heavenly life or metempsychosis, they have largely skirted around the invincible mystery of the passage. The belief in resurrection is too quick and too simplistic in saying that the fact of death is nothing but a passage ending in another form of life for the soul or something or other, whereas it is an impenetrable totality, an end, an unfathomable breach. It is curious, moreover, to observe just how much Christianity and Buddhism, despite their radical differences, would in a sense agree on the idea of a passage, of another life.

Must we not admit that the faith in a revelation or a belief, whatever it may be, is nevertheless not an answer or a postmortem guarantee? Nothing, no promise of eternal life, can elucidate the mystery of death. The question Kafka poses is fundamental: "Is it possible to think something that is inconsolable? Or rather something that is inconsolable without the shadow of a consolation?"[1] But the heavens are desperately empty and silent, even threatening. We recall Perken at the end of *The Royal Way* crying out "that no hope of heaven, no promise of reward, nothing can justify the end of any human life."[2]

The lasting quality of the impenetrable character of death is not necessarily a negation of faith, nor even a danger for the believer. It is simply that this question asserts that it is in the power of no god, no prophet, no messiah to answer. And yet how many religions have tended to monopolize the mystery of death, as if they alone possessed the key? Indeed, who can deny that the in-itself of the objectivity of our relation to death is impenetrability? In the *Logical Investigations,* Husserl writes, "How shall we understand that the *in itself* of objectivity reaches *representation,* and thus could again become in some sense subjective?" (*GCM* 20).

It is similar for those who proclaim that after death there is Nothing. I want to reread here the words Levinas said to me during one of our meetings and which forcefully state the problematic we are dealing with:

> Initially one says that death is negation. But it's not a negation, since it's a mystery. It's not at all that there's no life after death, that there's no hope for

---

1. [Translated from Kafka, *Oeuvres complètes* 3:441. This diary entry, dated October 19, 1917, does not appear in the English translation of the *Diaries of Franz Kafka.* —Trans.]

2. See Malraux, *The Royal Way,* 249.

Dialogue with Malraux 71

survival, for resurrection. The resurrection also says too simplistically that death is nothing. What it is, we simply don't know, because it's a mystery par excellence. To speak of death is to abandon all logic. It's not just a question of the fact that we die. All the logical forms we would use to circumscribe death disappear in the event we're trying to describe.[3]

The question is knowing whether an authentic faith is compatible with being objective toward the questions posed by death. The faith of revealed religions, nourished by its own essentially subjective truths, is more often than not incapable of replying to the slightest certainties of the unbeliever, whether a skeptic or an agnostic. In *Lazarus,* Malraux reflects on the invincible mystery of death, in other words, on the question of knowing whether its enigma can ever be elucidated. "The revelation is that nothing can be revealed."[4] But what was Malraux thinking of exactly when he wrote this striking thought? Given the context of the book, what was he thinking of other than the unthinkable of death that "has neither shape nor name"? It can in no way be a question here, as some would have us believe, of religious Revelation, which Malraux used to write with a capital letter. Can we not try to go further in our reasoning and assert that the phrase "nothing can be revealed" is already the beginning of a revelation on death? A paradoxical revelation that there is nothing to reveal.

The objectivity that the question of death forces upon us is or should be inherent in the subjectivity of faith, like a gaping hole. Death is in essence a breaking up, the rupture of being, of continuity, consciousness, the end of times. In itself, death is unthinkable, and it is this objectivity

3. See above, p. 26.
4. Malraux, *Lazarus,* 147.

with which we are trying to concede the unthinkable that forces us momentarily to rid ourselves of the speculations of faith. Death essentially refutes the idea of something implicit. It is only in a dialogue with nothing implicit that we can begin to understand one another. Do we know any more of God than we do of death? Such is the question of relativity—not of faith but of the feeling that all too often leads believers to presume they possess the entire truth. "About God we know nothing. But this not-knowing is a not-knowing about God. As such, it is the beginning of our knowledge about him," wrote Franz Rosenzweig in 1918 when he began the first book of *Der Stern der Erlösung* [*The Star of Redemption*],[5] a book we know was of fundamental importance to Levinas, and in particular for the end of the idea of Totality. This proposition is the very bedrock of the concept of the nonimplicit that presides over the possibility of a fraternal dialogue between believers and agnostics or atheists. "About death we know nothing. As such, this not-knowing is the beginning of our knowledge about it." Is there not a connection between Rosenzweig's words and Malraux's thought about the absolute enigma of death: "the revelation is that nothing can be revealed"?

In his last academic series of lectures (1975–1976), given at the Sorbonne and entitled "Death and Time," Emmanuel Levinas proposes an extremely striking analysis of death (*GDT* 7–117).[6]

If I wanted to show in the previous chapter that behind Levinas's silence on Kafka there was nevertheless, as the

---

5. Rosenzweig, *The Star of Redemption*, 31.
6. [In fact, this was only one of two lecture courses Levinas gave that year, the other being entitled "God and Onto-Theology" (*GDT* 121–224).—Trans.]

rare words he devoted to him prove, a proximity to the point of the very impossibility of saying more about him, is there not too in Malraux's fundamental impossibility of mentioning Kafka an unsayable link with the world's absurdity such as the genius from Prague understood it and in the quasi-mystical way he expressed it? In his *Diary,* Kafka notes, "'If...you will die' means that knowledge is both the stage leading to eternal life and the obstacle that bars access to that life."[7] Would there be a contradiction therefore between the idea of nonrevelation and the idea that nothing can be revealed? This is not just a matter of prolepsis. It is as if we were seized and overtaken by the ultimate meaning of these words. The thought expressed in *Lazarus* never ceases to surprise or to question its readers, believers or not, for its metaphysical or atheological positions, and especially when Malraux refers to death and to nothing else. We would have expected him to write, as an agnostic, that "the revelation is that there is nothing to reveal," yet as we said he writes that nothing can be revealed. Does this text not take us to the very heart of the issue, if not to say aporia, for these words can paradoxically mean that something is to be revealed but cannot be? A question we find in Kafka. And if this "something or other" were to belong to death in its infrangible enigma, then does this mean that it belongs to death alone, or would there be in Malraux's thought only the premise of the possibility of a revelation that would not be of the sole domain of utopia, as if the ultimate secret of death is that there is no secret? We are in the very domain of transcendence,

---

7. Kafka, *Diaries of Franz Kafka,* entry dated January 28, 1918. [Translated from Saint Cheron's modified version of Kafka's entry in *Oeuvres complètes* 3:469.—Trans.]

of "what escapes man" or, to put it differently, of "what human knowledge has no grasp of."[8] What is certain is that for Malraux there was a profound difference between being agnostic and being an atheist, seeing agnosticism as a kind of intellectual equivalent to faith, at least in the sense in which agnosticism does not initially rule out the possibility of faith but acknowledges not having been seized by it. In the television documentary *La légende du siècle* [*Legend of the Century*], Malraux said,

> To be agnostic means to think that there is no possible link between human thought and the conception of an absolute transcendence. This doesn't mean you're an atheist because to be an atheist means saying that transcendence is false, it doesn't exist. I don't think at all that transcendence doesn't exist. I think it exists in a fundamental way and that men are only men when they are in relation to transcendence, which can take many forms and is not necessarily religious. The great figures of humanity are all linked to a form of transcendence.[9]

If Levinas had been aware of these words, would he not have felt some proximity with the author of *Man's Fate*, with whom he shared with such conviction the thought—so much more than an idea!—that one can "die for the other"? These words are the very essence of the "empirical apperception," to use Kant's language, that Malraux had of agnosticism as a reality. In 1974 he clarified yet further his profound thought on the question:

> I believe that between the nature of knowledge and the fact of transcendence, there is an absolute break.

---

8. Malraux, *Les métamorphoses du regard*.
9. Malraux, *La légende du siècle*.

Which means that I am an absolute agnostic, no more or less, moreover, than Saint Thomas who said that "religion exists through faith alone." So if you have faith, you have faith, and if you don't have it, then all rational attempt is doomed to failure. The order of transcendence is not of the order of intelligence.[10]

Who would deny that death is a mystery? But who would doubt too that it is a part of biological life? Does that make it more acceptable? That agnosticism is appropriate for Malraux does not mean that he believed in nothingness. On the contrary, he opposed nothingness with the unthinkable of death and conceived of agnosticism as capable of experiencing the "unthinkable with the strength of faith." The same idea can be found in Levinas when he writes that "death is not identical to nothingness. The human being is thus a way of not being-to-death" (*GDT* 55). But for a different reason altogether.

I remember Levinas's reply one day when I asked him about death as the question par excellence, the question that precedes and leads to all the others: "When I say that death is not nothingness, I'm in no way implying an opposition between being and nothingness. Not that there is an excluded third party, but *as if there were* an excluded third party. To think nothingness and not being, is not the same thing."[11]

In this question, according to Levinas, there is an "irresolvable alternative in death between being and not being. But there is certainly something else:...an alternative between this alternative and an excluded

---

10. Malraux, "Radioscopie de Jacques Chancel."
11. See above, pp. 26–27.

unthinkable third, through which death precisely is a mystery, an unknown beyond."[12] Is this the issue Malraux tried to have his contemporaries and above all future generations avoid when on the second to last page of *Lazarus,* which closes *The Mirror of Limbo,* he asks himself what would happen if in future times, "in the presence of men ready to listen at last, the ultimate prophet were to yell at Death: 'There is no extinction!'"[13]

This exclamation testifies to an undeniable proximity of thought with Levinas whose attachment to the Hebrew texts and traditions of the synagogue, no matter how faithful, has not stopped some people from suspecting him of having an agnostic religious turn of mind, as opposed to Malraux's more religious agnostic turn of mind. Would we have forgotten Malraux's definition of the term "unknowable," which "insidiously suggests a knowledge that is never attained but that would extend ours?"[14] What does he mean?

Some have seen in Malraux's work an immense dirge, a song of mourning, whereas on the contrary it is an inexhaustible song to the mystery of life, to the mystery of the "first smile of the first child." The obsession with death needs to be understood as the reverse side of the obsession with life. At almost 75 years of age, in the sublime and final pages of *L'homme précaire et la littérature* [*Precarious Man and Literature*], Malraux writes that "death is an invincible mystery; life a strange mystery."[15] The two mysteries come together in one single

---

12. Levinas, "Amour et révélation," 142.
13. Malraux, *Lazarus,* 148.
14. Ibid., 143.
15. Malraux, *L'homme précaire et la littérature,* 326.

quest for meaning, as with all of his work. To evoke death, everywhere at all times, like the famous sting, was the means Malraux employed to better celebrate life, for it is in deepening the mystery of the dark, of the realm of night, that life takes on its irreducible miraculous dimension.

THE EPIPHANY OF LIFE

There is an incessant question in Levinas of the justification for living which becomes tragic insofar as it carries in its most intimate conscience the "unjustified privilege" of having survived six million deaths: "Is it righteous to be?" This haunting and tragic questioning is certainly absent from Malraux, even if deep down his work is also a question of the justification of life. Kyo embodies this questioning in *Man's Fate:* "What would have been the value of a life for which he would not have been willing to die?"[16] But both he and his characters know, moreover, the feeling of original stupefaction before the fact of being, which explains his fascination with those moments of the return to life after the approach of death, such as the cyclone after returning from the expedition he made by plane in 1934 over Yemen, when he was looking for the Queen of Sheba's capital in the company of his friend Captain Corniglion-Molinier, or the return from the tank trap in 1940, and the serious illness in 1972 related in *Lazarus.* Malraux transcribes each return to life as if he were evoking biblical times, contemporaneous with the garden of Eden in which the original Adam, in other words, primordial man, could contemplate "the first smile

---

16. Malraux, *Man's Fate,* 304.

of the first child." This time in which everything appears to us as if for the first time is the time of Genesis, as Sergio Villani has magnificently shown.[17] It is not the word of God, but the epiphany of the human face and the slightest trace of humanity which, with each return like so many repetitions of a unique rebeginning, reveal life in a similar sense to the Revelation. The agnostic Malraux and the practicing Jew Levinas come together by way of a word that is fundamental to both of them, the word "epiphany." Each return to earth for Malraux was an epiphany, and Levinas's entire ethical philosophy is predicated on "the epiphany of the face."

At the end of the *Mirror of Limbo* there is a paragraph that is, at the least, absolutely crucial:

> My memory, it has been said, dwells upon my returns to earth, after the cyclone or tank trap and the events of the Vistula, Spain, and the Resistance—moments that represent epiphanies. The metamorphosis of ignorance of death into awareness of death, the metamorphosis of knowledge into belief—these, surely, belong to the realm of epiphanies? My odyssey outside the earth to bring back the tablets is also an obscure epiphany. The revelation is that nothing can be revealed. The unknown realm of the unthinkable has neither shape nor name.[18]

Was *Lazarus* the first book in which Malraux resorted to the word "epiphany"?

Each and every "return to life" prior to Malraux's hospitalization at the Salpêtrière stigmatizes in some way the epiphanies of light, all deriving from the experience

---

17. See Villani, "Malraux-Israël."
18. Malraux, *Lazarus,* 147.

Malraux had lived through on his feet, so to speak, when he was master of his destiny. But in *Lazarus* he underwent the experience, since for the first time the approach of death came not from an external phenomenon but from within: medicine and biology alone could work here. In the book Malraux wrote recollecting the approach of death, we understand without hesitation that the "returns to earth" clearly "represent epiphanies." Does Emmanuel Levinas's work, from *Totality and Infinity* to *Alterity and Transcendence,* one of his last books, throw light, unwittingly and unintentionally, on the image of Lazarus? Have we misunderstood both of them, or worse, extrapolated their respective thoughts? What I am trying to see in the fundamental experience Malraux went through is an ethics taking shape. That the philosopher of ethics should encounter in Malraux's pages, other than his life story, a writer who wanted "to make men conscious of their grandeur" is not unimportant, even if the encounter is concentrated around a few words. But let us acknowledge at least that the encounter is situated at the pinnacle of profound thought, for the words in question are so intense that one cannot pass them without stopping. No doubt for the beginning of a dialogue to take place I had to get to know, after my acquaintance with André Malraux, the exceptional mentor that was Emmanuel Levinas, one of the leading lights of philosophy and thought at the end of this millennium and whose genius was to have given a positive meaning to culpability and to have made of ethics not a branch of philosophy but the first philosophy.

Let us tackle the following lines from *Totality and Infinity:* "The epiphany of the face qua face opens humanity...in the eyes that look at me....The epiphany of the face is ethical" (*TI* 213, 199). And in *Otherwise Than Being or Beyond Essence:* "The transcendence of the revelation lies in the fact that the 'epiphany' comes in the saying of him that received it" (*OB* 149).

These two passages demonstrate the heights to which Levinas raises the epiphany. It is more than an apparition, it resembles a revelation in that it "reveals" the infinite, as he goes on to say. With "the epiphany of the face," Levinas does not simply see the person as is, because he knows that the human face bears within it the trace and the reflection of humanity, of the infinite.

In the Nazi extermination camps, as in the execution center at Tuol Sleng in Cambodia, both transformed today into memorial museums—and perhaps in the memorial museums of tomorrow in Rwanda or the former Yugoslavia—every photograph of a face exhibited to the public represents dozens, indeed hundreds of thousands of victims who disappeared, for many, without a trace. In this sense every human face bears the presence of the world within it. In Levinas's metaphysics, in the beginning was the face and the face was inseparable from an ethical word, from being chosen.

If, for Levinas, "the epiphany of the face qua face opens humanity," then the epiphany of life, after leaving the tank trap, also opens up Malraux to humanity. So we will not have opened the breach in vain.

The extraordinary final pages of *The Walnut Trees of Altenburg* are to the novel what the final pages of *The Voices of Silence* and the last page of *The Intemporal* are to Malraux's books about art. Each of these endings has something in common with the ending of *An die Freude* of Beethoven's *Ninth Symphony,* or the first movement of Brahms's *First Symphony,* or Bach's *Et expecto* in his *Messe en Si*.

An impetuous, lively style coupled with cosmic, almost biblical images in which earth, heaven, and the elements all have a part in the score. It is the struggle between fundamental anguish and the no less fundamental exultation that precedes it perhaps in the garden of Eden of our dreams, before man understands he will die. The words Malraux uses in *The Walnut Trees* to express his return to earth overflow with a powerful religious sentiment: "But this morning, I am all birth.... from that night there rises the miraculous revelation of day.... this life which, this morning for the first time, has shown itself as powerful as the darkness and as powerful as death."[19]

Malraux will rarely have gone so far in order to signify a decisive experience whose effect—the revelation of the light of life—somewhat eclipses its cause, namely falling into the trap. Malraux writes, unambiguously, "I can scarcely remember what fear is like; what I carry within me is the discovery of a simple, sacred secret. Thus, perhaps, did God look at the first man."[20]

His intense feeling of having been brought back to life, a true cenesthesia of the soul, calls out to the resurrection of the earth, in "the dazzling mystery of the morning." There is a feeling of being seized by a form of transcendence in this text, but it is not the Word of God, Malraux recognizes, rather, it is the epiphany of a voiceless humanity revealing to him not that "in the beginning God created heaven and earth," but that the "in the beginning created Elokim."[21] Again, Levinas and Malraux seem to be on the same powerful wavelength with this image of a before-days, this biblical dawn in which Eve stands opposite Adam, not in her nakedness but as a face.

---

19. Malraux, *The Walnut Trees of Altenburg*, 222–23.
20. Ibid., 224.
21. See Zaklad, *Pour une éthique*.

The face is alone in translating transcendence. Not to provide the proof of the existence of God, but the indispensable circumstance of the meaning of that word, of its first statement. Of the first prayer, of the first liturgy. A Transcendence that is inseparable from the ethical *circumstances* of the responsibility for the other, in which the thought of the unequal is thought.... But, as non-transferable responsibility, it has received its uniqueness of self from the epiphany of the face. (*OS* 94–95)

How could one deny that the entire ending of *The Walnut Trees* has an indisputable ring to it of the "first liturgy," that the epiphany of the face is at the heart of the revelation Malraux felt or sensed in this "biblical dawn"? Indeed, it takes little for what still seemed central to him a few moments earlier to falter and for the indisputable ethical feeling to remind him that "the mystery of man only emerge[s] from that enigmatic smile, and the resurrection of the earth becomes nothing more than a pulsating backcloth."[22] Malraux always comes back to the mystery of man, for the world, life, God himself, are but Man. What is it to rediscover life, if it is not to rediscover the human?

Lazarus is also "the epiphany of the unthinkable," the most singular approach of death that Malraux knew, for as we said, it was something he underwent and had not mastered since the enemy this time came from within, lurking inside him, in the very depths of his being, impossible to dislodge because inherent in what it actually is, life itself. In his room in the Salpêtrière hospital, it was not God Malraux saw face to face without dying, since this is an impossibility, as Moses teaches us in a

---

22. Malraux, *The Walnut Trees of Altenburg*, 224.

paradigmatic verse in the book of Exodus (33:20). The God of Israel—God of Jesus and of Muhammad—had said to him, "You will not be able to see my face, for no human can see My face and live." It is death Malraux contemplated, in other words, the "obscure epiphany." But have we not already asked this question, namely, whether God and death are the same, except that death, in its immanence, would be more familiar to us than God himself in his transcendence, in his absence, indeed in his "nonrevelation"? Twice Malraux really came face to face with death, at Gramat in front of the firing squad, and at the Salpêtrière hospital some 30 years later. Both were very real. Compared to these experiences, the cyclone on his return from Sheba and the tank trap were more like encounters with mortal anguish than with death as such.

We have to come back here to the central paragraph at the end of the *Mirror of Limbo:* "My odyssey outside the earth to bring back the tablets is also an obscure epiphany. The revelation is that nothing can be revealed. The unknown realm of the unthinkable has neither shape nor name."[23]

What does it mean to assert that the revelation is shapeless and nameless, that nothing can be revealed? We may well wonder whether we are dealing with a religious revelation, in the widest sense, or with a revelation in the unique domain of death, in other words, is there no empirical knowledge of death? It is certainly a question of death, but failing a revelation Malraux, like certain other people, was only allowed to know "an obscure epiphany." Malraux would never have gotten so close to what again

---

23. Malraux, *Lazarus,* 147.

in *Lazarus* he calls "the boundless depths foretokening death."[24] It was at this point that he discovered a "state" he had previously "ignored," and the entire narrative is built on the premise of the unknown. No more lyricism from the miraculous survivor of the tank trap, or for having returned from Sheba, but a purified narrative in its attempt to delimit and isolate as closely and as much as possible the limit experience from which he had returned. "The death in the ceruse mask" that Saint-John Perse sings about in *Song for an Equinox* lurks around the whole episode. Malraux's hospital roommate dies, and what follows his own return is a "terrible state of limbo."

What *Lazarus* teaches in the end is the contagious, almost Buddhist serenity with which Malraux speaks of death in the final lines. His agnosticism, as we have shown, was not at all a notion that denied transcendence all reality. Quite the opposite. The "god" he could not believe in is a god that could only be apprehended by the sacredness of a theophany or an incarnation. One suspects the interest he could have nurtured for a work such as Emmanuel Levinas's. This attempt—temptation indeed—to demonstrate some of the points of convergence between the two works has struck a number of thinkers over the last few years.[25]

Levinas's thought on God could be described as being agnostic, a-religious, or a desacralized religion predicated rather on holiness, the ultimate goal of all true relation between a human being and the Totally Other. For Levinas, the God of Israel, of the Bible, is a fundamentally

---

24. Ibid., 85.
25. See the studies by Boblet-Viart, "Roman 20–50"; Levy, *André Malraux;* and Zarader, *Malraux ou la pensée.*

ethical God, revealed in the face of the other more than in rituals or in quiet communion with him.

> I always thought that the invisible God of monotheism is not only a God who is not visible to the eyes. It is a nonthematizable God. When can a positive sense be given to this negative notion? When I am turned toward the other man and when I am called not to leave him alone. It is a turning contrary to my perseverance in being. This is the circumstance in which God has spoken. (*IRB* 101)

Malraux would have found more than one analysis, more than one approach close to his own preoccupations in *Totality and Infinity,* Levinas's magisterial essay on exteriority. Levinas writes:

> A relation with the Transcendent free from all captivation by the Transcendent is a social relation. It is here that the Transcendent, infinitely other, solicits us and appeals to us. The proximity of the Other, the proximity of the neighbor, is in being an ineluctable moment of the revelation of an absolute presence (that is, disengaged from every relation), which expresses itself. (*TI* 78)

Extending this analysis, Levinas goes on to broach the atheism of the philosopher, and what he says could well have been written for the agnostic:

> The atheism of the metaphysician means, positively, that our relation with the Metaphysical is an ethical behavior and not theology, not a thematization, be it a knowledge by analogy, of the attributes of God. God rises to his supreme and ultimate presence as correlative to the justice rendered unto men. (*TI* 78)

Hence the fundamental idea that if God is the absolute unknowable, then human holiness is that by which God is *present* in the world, insofar as the human is the very locus and impassable limit of this presence. For Emmanuel Levinas, ethics is not the path toward the Totally Other, it is the absolute locus in which transcendence becomes epiphany.

On the very first page of what is considered Levinas's philosophical masterpiece, *Otherwise Than Being or Beyond Essence,* he writes the following fundamental lines that serve as the foundation of an entirely new transcendence distinct from Saint Augustine's, Kant's, even Bergson's:

> If transcendence has meaning, it can only signify the fact that the *event of being, the esse, the essence,* passes over to what is other than being.... To be or not to be is not the question where transcendence is concerned. The statement of being's *other,* of the otherwise than being, claims to state a difference over and beyond that which separates being from nothingness—the very difference of the *beyond,* the difference of transcendence. (*OB* 3)

Levinas's transcendence, then, passes through the *otherwise than being.* This vision of transcendence is not simply worked out in intellectual or philosophical terms; strictly speaking, it is the incarnation of Revelation. Which is why we can speak of the descent of God "in the guise of" the face of the other as in the form of putting into practice the commandment to love, received from and bearing witness to a God of love preexistent to the New Testament.

> The Other is the very locus of metaphysical truth, and is indispensable for my relation with God. He does not play the role of a mediator. The Other is not the incarnation of God, but precisely by his face, in which he is disincarnate, is the manifestation of the height in which God is revealed. (*TI* 78–79)

Although for Malraux faith belonged to the order of transcendence alone, more than to ethics, he was sensitive his whole life and throughout his work to the act being appropriate to the Word of the Jewish and Christian Revelation. His fierce determination not to be a believer comes from his nature as a born rebel. Rebellious to the whole idea of a God and perhaps even more so to God's incarnation.

As a philosopher, Levinas is not afraid to write in his work *Entre Nous:*

> Can the God who humbles Himself to "dwell with the contrite and the humble" (Isaiah 57:15), the God "of the stranger, the widow, and the orphan," the God manifesting Himself in the world... can He, in His excessiveness, become a *present* in the time of the world? Isn't that too much for His poverty? Is it not too little for His glory without which His poverty is not a humiliation? (*EN* 56–57)

As an agnostic, Malraux was no less deeply sensitive, from *The Temptation of the West* to *Precarious Man*—that is, over 50 years of writing—to reading the divine trace in the human face. But there is one other level on which Malraux and Levinas would have met, on which their work does meet, namely that in the Jewish philosopher, steeped in Talmud and Torah, there is "the idea of a God without divinity, of a religion without piety" (Solomon Malka, in *IRB* 101).

In *Totality and Infinity,* Levinas broaches the fundamental question, which can be read as the essence of his own religious position: "To relate to the absolute as an atheist is to welcome the absolute purified of the violence of the sacred" (*TI* 77). Although the first-person singular is not used here, one feels that the understanding with which Levinas apprehends the atheist clearly indicates his own refusal of the sacred because of the violence and idolatry it possesses or can possess. The greatness of Judaism for Levinas comes precisely from having destroyed the idols, having refused false gods and false messiahs, and having opposed sacredness with holiness. But it is an opposition that always has to be begun anew, at the risk of idolizing the ritual prohibitions that hold back Jewish universality.

MAN AGAINST DEATH

Parallel to this fundamental approach to the signification of the transcendent and transcendence, Malraux and Levinas would have come together on one additional major point, which we have already hinted at: namely the question of death. In his *Malraux par lui-même* [*Malraux by Himself*], Gaëtan Picon seems to take sides with Sartre when he writes, "No doubt Sartre was right in saying that for Malraux, as for Heidegger, man is a 'being-for-death,'" *Sein-zum-Tode,* to use the German philosopher's expression. In the margins of Picon's text, Malraux had written, "And what if, instead of saying for, one said against? It's only apparently the same thing."[26]

In a striking page from *Totality and Infinity,* Levinas opposes Heidegger when he writes, "Time is precisely the fact that the whole existence of the mortal being—exposed to violence—is not being for death, but the 'not yet' which is a way of being against death, a retreat before death in the very midst of its inexorable approach" (*TI* 224). If these lines constitute a refutation, a challenge to the great German philosopher's *Sein-zum-Tode,*

---

26. Picon, *Malraux par lui-même,* 74.

they also indicate an incredible proximity of thought with Malraux, as if this proximity had been waiting for these lines in order to reveal itself.

The difference between the for and against is an irreducible one, and Sartre himself was a philosopher of the *zum-Tode,* as opposed to Levinas, who was primarily a philosopher of the *gegen-Tode,* the against-death. This proximity is all the more astonishing and unexpected for being ignored during Malraux and Levinas's lifetime.

Even if this kinship beyond the grave were to stop with the fierce determination to set the human against death, to refuse to want to see in the human but a *Sein-zum-Tode,* it would be no less extraordinary. But if, for Malraux, it was eminently artistic Creation that set man against inexorable fatality, it was also the fraternity not only of the dead but of the living. Levinas called this fraternity ethics. He refused to see it as a branch of philosophy; quite the contrary, it was the first philosophy.

Through fraternity and art, which as forms of anti-destiny are the keys to his work, Malraux denies death the final victory, as if death only apparently had the last word. Was it in order to give death some positive meaning, or to take away its implacable sting and the putrid stench that accompanies it—both thinkers having already dismissed the idea that death gives on to nothingness? Such is and will be the human question par excellence for as long as there are human beings on earth.

We thus move closer to the question of the meaning of life. If it is true that the question of death is not the ultimate question but the first, the one that determines all the others, as Levinas puts it, the question of the meaning of life is measured on the basis of the question of death. It is therefore on the basis of every individual's response to his or her own mortality, and to that of others, that life has or has not meaning. The originality and the force of Levinas's thought lie in having linked the question of death to the question of ethics. In his opposition to Heidegger, he translates them into a refutation of "everyone dies for himself," for which he substitutes a "dying for the other."

For Malraux, fraternity, "as strong as death," constitutes one of the quests for the absolute, a dimension of heroism to the point of holiness, to the point of the "taking upon oneself of the dying for the other" (*GCM* 163) which embodies for Levinas the moment in which *God comes to mind*.

4

Otherwise than Thinking: A Philosophy of the Breach

WHAT IS THAT—THINKING? To this initial question let us add the question that opens Heidegger's book *What Is That—Philosophy?* On the first page of the book, it will be remembered, the German philosopher recalls Gide's words that "it is with beautiful feelings, that bad literature is made."[1] "Feelings," Heidegger continues, "even the most beautiful feelings, do not belong in philosophy. Feelings, people say, are something irrational. Philosophy, on the other hand, is not only something rational but is the true end and proper administration of *ratio*."[2] Following which, Heidegger poses a whole series of questions, including this one: "Has *ratio* constituted herself the mistress of

---

1. Cited by Heidegger, *What Is That—Philosophy?*, 4–5.
2. Ibid., 5.

philosophy? If the answer is 'yes,' by what right? If 'no,' whence does she receive her charge and her role?"[3] We all know that the word "philosophy" comes from the ancient Greek φιλοσοφια, made up of φιλειν, "to love" and σοφια, "wisdom, knowledge," in other words, literally, "the love of wisdom." But how often do we reflect on the entire amphibology the word "philosophy" contains, as soon as it is pronounced, on the problematic inherent in and constituted by its etymology? The "love of wisdom" disappeared early on for so many didactic philosophers who were quick to replace it with the "love of knowing" or the "quest for wisdom" or the "quest for knowledge," as if to signify that the wisdom of love was not on a level with true philosophy. But let us look at the differences in reading in more detail, since *philosophia* can signify in contradictory fashion "love of wisdom" (*Liebe zur Weisheit*) as well as "love of knowledge" (*Liebe zum Wissen*) or "desire for knowledge" in an Aristotelian optic. In this respect, Levinas breaks with Aristotle, Plato, and the majority voice of an entire panoply of Western philosophers, right up to Heidegger, of course, but also Adorno, who privileged the love of knowledge over the "wisdom of love," thus revolutionizing in a sense the image we have of philosophy. If σοφια is indeed wisdom, possibly also "knowledge," then φιλειν, which qualifies *sophia,* becomes so to speak its attribute: the essence of wisdom is to elicit love, according to Levinas's teaching.

Let us start by noting that philosophy is neither Chinese nor Indian, Jewish nor Arabic, even if later there was above all an extremely potent Jewish and Arab

---

3. Ibid., 5.

philosophy in the Middle Ages, as well as brilliant schools of thought in India and China.

The twentieth century saw an efflorescence of philosophers on the soil of Old Europe where two world wars were to be perpetrated, with their millions of deaths and one of the greatest tragedies of humanity: the Holocaust or Shoah, the extermination of six million European Jews, so linked was the Polish Jewish community to Poland's own tragedy. To this one can add other nameless tragedies such as the Armenian and Cambodian genocides, the genocide of the Tutsis at the close of the century, or the great Stalinist purges as well as those ordered by Mao and his Red Guard during the Cultural Revolution.

Emmanuel Levinas was 22 years old when in 1928–1929 at the University of Freiburg he attended Edmund Husserl's last lectures and discovered the phenomenology that would mark his entire thought. For Levinas, Husserl's words and his work opened up a nontheoretical intentionality that could not be reduced to knowledge; his last two classes in particular dealt with the notion of phenomenological psychology and the constitution of intersubjectivity.

But it was his discovery of Heidegger's *Sein und Zeit* that transfigured his philosophical life and his life as such, even if he would become increasingly critical of Heidegger from the latter's Nazi profession of faith onward. Nonetheless, he very soon placed *Being and Time* among the five masterpieces of Western philosophy, on a par with Plato's *Phaedrus,* Kant's *Critique of Pure Reason,* Hegel's *Phenomenology of Mind,* and Bergson's *Time and Free Will.* After this discovery of the idea of intentionality of consciousness, the young phenomenologist understood that "being commands the access to being. The access to being belongs to the description of being"

(*EI* 31). After this, the consciousness of a "fundamental ontology" harbored by the term "being" in Heidegger was a revelation for him.

What interests me here—as much as my modest means allow me—is to develop the philosophical and phenomenological process that Levinas constructed through diachrony, inasmuch as it presupposes and announces the primacy of the otherwise than being, which is constitutive of a radical breach in the order of being with the traditional conception of time,[4] even if it means breaking with Bergson's already innovative duration. I simply would like to succeed in showing, in a succinct analysis, how Levinas's fascination for "the ontological problem of being" discovered in Heidegger will give birth to one of the most critical, indeed heretical works of contemporary philosophy, in the name of an ethics that is not totalitarian as some would have us believe, but simply a first principle.

At the beginning of the 1930s, Levinas gives us his *Reflections on the Philosophy of Hitlerism* in which he develops his first analyses of freedom, liberalism, Marxism. Behind these analyses is the entire critique of racism, of the extreme danger of the return to the Same, of the suppression of the Other and his or her diabolization, denounced by the young Levinas in his critique of both National Socialist politics and the Marxist politics at work in Stalin's Soviet Union, two regimes of absolute terror. What is in danger here, beyond the problematic of freedom introduced by the French Enlightenment and the German *Aufklärung,* is the biblical Judeo-Christian

---

4. See the remarkable analysis of diachrony by Calin and Sebbah in *Le vocabulaire de Levinas.*

heritage, and above all, Levinas says, "the very humanity of man."⁵

Heir to this double philosophical and biblical heritage, spoken on the one hand in Hebrew and Aramaic, and on the other in Greek, Latin, German, and French, Levinas proved faithful to the Platonic tradition of the "Good beyond being" familiar to Bergson, following on from Descartes, Pascal, Kant, and Husserl. But this heritage also eminently encounters Hegel, whose powerful *Phenomenology of Mind* left its profound mark on both his direct followers and his opponents. Evidently, the principle of totality and a theory of history had to be laid down in order for them to be criticized! Levinas's fidelity to the Platonic tradition also goes hand in hand with a resistance, a fierce opposition to the primacy of ontology that dominated Western thought and philosophy.

Let us presuppose then that Levinas's entire work responds to Heidegger's initial question—which is not "What Is That—Philosophy?" but rather "the question of the signification of being, as verb" (*EI* 38)—with another question: is a philosophy that is only a fundamental ontology still a philosophy? To some ears, the question may seem blunt, blasphemous even. Everyone knows that it is not enough to know what philosophy is in order to be capable of doing something with it that has tangible human meaning. Of course, it is from within philosophy and not outside its field of application that Levinas poses his question and seeks to posit a breach—a breach against indifference—a critique in relation to a tradition of the Greek logos that has been more preoccupied with the veiling of being than with the veiling of the other of

---

5. Levinas, "Reflections on the Philosophy of Hitlerism," 71.

being, the Platonic "Good beyond being" and, finally, the "otherwise-than-being."

We are opening up a crucial question here. Levinas thinks responsibility and the very diachrony of time as constituent data guaranteeing not pure knowledge or pure thought or even pure philosophy—self-sufficient perhaps and in the agora still cut off from the world—but a theoretical knowledge giving way to the act, to its practicality, for one is never in tune with a philosophy that thinks itself as "otherwise-than-being," out of reach of the diachrony that carries within it the world's entire sociality, like an impossible indifference to the other.

A noesis, in other words the act of thinking, that would make do with its noema, the intentional object of thought, would end up, according to the philosopher—if I understand him correctly—in sterile, dried-out theoretical knowledge. Is it this balance precisely, this dialectic—an urgent imperative too—between phenomenology and the concrete, that always places this work on the edges, in the borders, at the boundary between philosophy and some abyss of holiness? Levinas runs the risk of being permanently on the borderline, at the very limit of what is tolerated by the upholders of an orthodoxy who like neither deviance nor reference to an order that is not specifically their own, such as the place Levinas accords the prophets[6] of Israel or certain talmudic sages and, even more so, the way he has recourse—such that his recourse becomes his very problematic, his mode of thought—to words of an order *other* than that of philosophy, such as holiness,

---

6. I refer here to the excellent page Michel Foucault devotes to the role of the prophet in *Le courage de la vérité,* his last class.

the epiphany of the face, or the "taking upon oneself of the ultimate gift of dying for another" (*GCM* 163). Levinas thus stands at the confines, the boundaries, the limits of a discourse that lays claim to belonging entirely to the philosophical. Hence the need for us to go through Jacques Derrida, in the sense that he makes it necessary through his own questioning. Delving more thoroughly and in a brutally direct way—his analysis shocked Levinas—into the anti-Hegelianism of his elder—juxtaposed, no doubt rapidly, by some specialists, to Kierkegaard's—Derrida uses the words "protest" and "confrontation." A confrontation in particular "with the anti-Hegelianism of Feuerbach and above all of Jaspers, and with the latter's anti-Husserlianism too,"[7] two philosophers Levinas rarely quotes but no matter if, as the father of deconstruction points out, there may be a possible convergence between them. Raising a "contradiction in the system,"[8] Derrida goes so far as to question the meaning of what he sees as a necessity in Levinas:

> the necessity of lodging oneself within traditional conceptuality in order to destroy it. Why did this necessity finally impose itself upon Levinas? Is it an extrinsic necessity? Does it not touch upon only an instrument, only an "expression," which can be put between quotation marks? Or does it hide, rather, some indestructible and unforeseeable resource of the Greek logos?[9]

---

7. Derrida in his important chapter "Violence and Metaphysics: An Essay on the Thought of Emmanuel Levinas," in *Writing and Difference,* 111. [Translation modified.—Trans.]
 8. Derrida, *Writing and Difference,* 111.
 9. Ibid., 111–12.

Through these questions Derrida attacks one of the striking aspects of Levinas's problematic embodied by and in a certain form of violence, willingly destroying with a view to reconstructing the Western speculative tradition which, with rare exceptions, was incapable for so long of passing over to the other of being, otherwise than being, and to hearing such a radical discourse on the face of the other man, which is also the face of the other woman. It is certainly important for Levinas to demonstrate that ethics alone has precellence over ontology, and as such constitutes the first philosophy and not a branch among others of the discipline; but, in order to do so, one needs to succeed in shaking the very foundations of philosophy. And who is capable of that? Derrida seems to have reproached "Levinas for being Levinas," to cite Jean-Luc Marion.

There is protest and confrontation then, but Derrida knew equally well that at the heart of Levinas's deconstructionist thought was the seed of a yet more crucial breach, dating from before the experience of the end of the world from 1940 to 1945—during which "god was truly dead or had gone back to his irrevelation" (*HO* 28)— a breach Levinas conceptualizes for the first time in 1946 in his series of lectures on *Time and the Other*. He closed his first lecture by putting forward a proposition of the greatest importance: "it is toward a pluralism that does not merge into unity that I should like to make my way and, if this can be dared, break with Parmenides" (*TO* 42). Why Parmenides? Because Parmenidian speculation ignores the alterity of the neighbor, ignores the other *qua* other. We now know how much Levinas's philosophical path presupposes, before even his exposition of the otherwise-than-being, a tearing away from the notion of being, of Heideggerian *Dasein*, and even more so from the major distinction in *Sein und Zeit* between the infinitive *Sein* and its present participle *Seiendes,* in other words, between *existing* and *existent.*

Emmanuel Levinas's phenomenological originality comes at the price of this tearing away, of this break with the notion of being, this break too with the entire philosophy of dialogue, of the I-Thou conceptualized by Buber and taken up by many philosophers, including Paul Ricoeur. The latter's *Oneself as Another* takes the exact opposite position to Levinas's discourse.

Levinas discovers Descartes' radical innovation of the thought of the infinite, from which years later will be born Levinas's concept and founding principle of the "epiphany of the face," for it is the face that the criminal or the executioner does not want to look at, wants to ignore in order better to destroy it or to torture it to death. It is starting from the consciousness of the infinite, the responsibility of the I and the irreducible uniqueness of the human being—and under the influence of Franz Rosenzweig and his *Star of Redemption* (1920)—that Levinas radically opposes Hegelian totality in particular. Faced with the death encountered on the battlefields of the Great War, Rosenzweig, who died in 1929, definitively broke with the principle of totality.

Evoking in 1982 the whole tragedy of our era—Hitlerism, Stalinism, Hiroshima, the Gulag, the genocides of Auschwitz and Cambodia—Levinas continues: "This is the century that is drawing to a close in the obsessive fear of the return of everything these barbaric names stood for: suffering and evil inflicted deliberately, but in a manner no reason set limits to, in the exasperation of a reason become political and detached from all ethics" (*EN* 97).

In 1961 came the publication of *Totality and Infinity: An Essay on Exteriority.* Having deepened his concept of responsibility and his notion of the epiphany of the face calling from within philosophy to go beyond it, where does the philosopher now stand? At this stage, we have to understand what the philosopher meant by the concept of exteriority. The kernel of this analysis of exteriority is the phenomenology of the face through a language that is still ontological—which will not be the case in *Otherwise Than Being or Beyond Essence* (1974). Primordial exteriority is not spatial but embodied by the other. True exteriority is alterity.

Reason sick with itself. That this era, laden with promises and aborted democratic dreams, beginning after World War Two and ending in 1970, after the quasi-planetary upheaval of 1968—of which one of the most tragic events was the crushing in August of the "Prague Spring" when Soviet tanks entered Prague, followed by Jan Palach, the 20-year-old philosophy student, setting himself on fire on January 19, 1969—that this era should have inspired Levinas's *Otherwise Than Being or Beyond Essence* is one of the nobler traces of what Western philosophical thought could leave during the last third of the twentieth century.

The working out of the metaphysics revealed in the book begins in the movement born from the phenomenology of the face—which is beyond a shadow of a doubt a metaphysics of alterity—and ends in a *meta*ethics. In *Otherwise Than Being,* however, the philosopher makes a decisive turn in his thought. The face is no longer alone at the center of phenomenology; it is the "responsibility" toward the other that defines the I and becomes the elementary cardinal axis of his analysis. There is certainly a speculative, metaphysical revelation at work here, a revelation of the other inasmuch as he or she summons me, calls me, obligates me. Levinas is not afraid to resort to the theological language he raises to a conceptual level by giving these words an unexpected universal dimension they lacked. We will come back to this.

Is exteriority at the beginning or at the end of the critique of totality, of the critique of ontology or, further still, of the critique of war with which the book opens? Is exiting from self the beginning of exteriority, of the precellence of the Other over the Same? What is it exactly that comes to oust being, the Same, the *conatus essendi,* Spinoza's being persevering in being, from self?

Is the beginning of exteriority what Levinas calls the "asymmetry of intersubjectivity"? To understand a little better the point here, one should recall the analysis Levinas gives of the intersubjective in *Existence and Existents,* written shortly after the war (1947).[10] In it we read:

> Intersubjective space is initially assymetrical. The exteriority of the other is not simply an effect of space, which keeps separate what conceptually is identical, nor is there some difference in the concepts which would manifest itself through spatial exteriority. It is precisely inasmuch as it is irreducible to these two notions of exteriority that social exteriority is an original form of exteriority and takes us beyond the categories of unity and multiplicity which are valid for things.... Intersubjectivity is not simply the application of the category of multiplicity to the domain of the mind. It is brought about by Eros. (*EE* 95)

---

10. [In fact, as Levinas makes clear in his prefatory note, this study was for the most part written in captivity in a German stalag during the war; see *EE* 15.—Trans.]

Eros is thus constitutive of intersubjectivity and perhaps already too of the asymmetry that exists between the I and the other in the erotic relationship. *Eros* is to be understood then in the guise of exteriority, as a category in its own right. Does the I, asks Levinas, not lose its "tragic egoity, returning to self," "in the guise of" this notion of fecundity? It appears clearly for the philosopher that the intersubjectivity of erotic love leads toward a beyond subjectivity, toward an exit from being that is already transcendence, for fecundity is inscribed in the depths of erotic desire, is an intrinsic part of it—even if modern sexuality is bent on separating desire and pleasure from fecundity. Subjectivity as it emerges from *Totality and Infinity* onward is a break with egoity; it is already hospitality and responsibility for the other.

Emmanuel Levinas's philosophy is carried by a thought "which carries all thought, [my] thought of the infinite, older than the thought of the finite, [which] is the very diachrony of time. It is noncoincidence, dispossession itself. This is a way of 'being dedicated' before any act of consciousness, and more deeply so than in consciousness, by way of the gratuity of time" (*GCM* xiv).

Our thinker, then, opposes the idea of totality with infinity, giving rise to an intricacy—an intrigue of the deepest kind, as it were—between totality, exteriority, the face of the other and infinity. The entire metaphysical intrigue of Levinas's thought is played out in these four words, these four events of Being. In *Totality and Infinity,* Levinas will definitively refute the idea of totality. Neither the "synthesis of knowledge [nor] the totality of being that is embraced by the *transcendental ego*" can be "the ultimate authorities in deciding what is *meaningful*" (*EN* 198), we read in the preface to the German edition of the book, dated 1987, in other words, 26 years after its first publication.

Levinas states from the outset that the idea of the relation to the infinite "is not a knowledge, but a Desire. I have tried to describe the difference between Desire and need by the fact that Desire cannot be satisfied; that Desire in some way nourishes itself on its own hungers and is augmented by its satisfaction; that Desire is like a thought which thinks more than it thinks, or more than what it thinks" (*EI* 92). In making this difference between Desire and need, Levinas opens up a second problematic, one concerning time, duration. Here is Bergson's powerful contribution. Need is inscribed in duration, is a part of it. The Desire that carries the infinite within it at the same time as it is carried by it is absolutely not erotic desire, which is the need for primary appeasement in the same way as hunger, thirst, or one's bodily functions. We are no longer in the order of need but in that of a voice coming from the depths of being and leading toward a beyond being. This Desire worries me, calls me, comes to me from the face of the other—which is also, as we will see when we conclude, the face of the third party, "in the face of the stranger, the widow and the orphan," an eminently biblical expression to which Levinas so frequently resorts in his philosophy—as if the only respectable philosophy or just philosophy possible was the one which starting from reason, saying, thinking, is concerned with the attention given precisely to the widow and the orphan. What is a philosophy that cares only for the same, for the self, without being possessed by the face of the defenseless? Without being *dis-possessed,* one should say more precisely. There is a *dispossession* of being, of the ego, in this inchoative responsibility for the other.

A metaphysics of temporality in its ethical signification, and one that does not forget Kant, whose "exaltation of theoretical reason into practical reason" Levinas praised.

It is important already to define the word "metaphysics" itself. Μέτα means "that which comes after" and φυσικά (*physiká*), "nature," in other words, "that which comes after the things of nature." It has to be said that Levinas's fundamental originality comes from the difference in approach to the initial question. The accusation Heidegger levies at metaphysics is that it has turned away from the thought of being *qua* being in order to privilege supreme beings. For Levinas, the difference was in the very origin of the μέτα of μέταφυσικά. For him, it is not a matter of linking the *after* to nature, nor to the physical, but to Being in its Being, thus inverting the perspective: what comes after Being, and thus after the ego, is the other in his or her radical alterity.

A discreet remark made by Heidegger in one of his Zollikon seminars underlines perfectly the insurmountable difference between himself and the philosopher of *Otherwise Than Being or Beyond Essence*. This is what he confided: "The impetus for my whole way of thinking goes back to an Aristotelian proposition which states that being is said in many ways. This proposition was originally the lightning bolt that triggered the question, What then is the unity of these various meanings of being? What does being mean at all?"[11] Levinas for his part is a Platonist, placing at the very foundation of philosophy the Good beyond Being.

In *Totality and Infinity*, Levinas creates a new concept, no doubt a little disconcerting at first, that of the "epiphany of the face." "Epiphany" comes from the Greek, meaning "manifestation." The epiphany of the face is thus the transcendent manifestation of Being, metaphysics, sociality. This transcendence is neither radiant nor glorious;

---

11. Heidegger, *Zollikon Seminars*, 119.

it takes place in the nakedness of the face of my neighbor, a defenseless face exposed to sickness, murder, death, calling in return for my responsibility, my intentional consciousness, my "love without concupiscence." Faced with this revelation of the other's face, the phenomenologist's discourse becomes more radical. In the last years of his life, when he had to write a preface for the German edition of his book, Levinas resorts to a vocabulary that is often foreign to the philosophical field but which he bends to give it a conceptual dimension. The word "holiness," for instance, which is not absent from the book, takes on a new tone in the new preface. How could he not broach, even if very rapidly, *Otherwise Than Being or Beyond Essence,* Levinas's masterly book in which he changes direction, delving into the abyss of the responsibility for the other to the point of turning myself into the other's hostage? A terrible paroxysmal, hyperbolic notion that no longer seems to be of the philosophical order at all but to belong to a different world order, a different order of thought. An "otherwise than thinking" that is literally an "Otherwise than being." Let's say that there is something radical in Levinas that disturbs, disconcerts, provokes, and, let's say it, has more than one of us shuddering, inciting some to pure and outright opposition. Ricoeur is one of the best examples of those philosophers who while sharing the same concern for responsibility, refuse Levinas's arguments. The philosopher of *Oneself as Another* criticizes the author of *Otherwise Than Being* for his "verbal terrorism,"[12] denounces the "trauma of substitution"—to use Jean-François Rey's words—called for by Levinas, and refuses to support the idea of the relation maintained by the traumatized ego with the third party in the return to justice.

---

12. Ricoeur, *Autrement,* 26.

Indeed, we may well wonder whether we are still in the philosophical domain with "the substitution for the other" or not already in some transcendent field that escapes all concept, all rationality of thought. We are certainly no longer in tune with the concept of responsibility since this notion exceeds all concepts, all philosophy, all metaphysics. Only saints are capable of substituting themselves for the other, not philosophers. Yet Levinas pursues his discourse in a vertiginous ascent toward a transcendent (not transcendental) metaphysics that leaves the researcher and reader "breathless." A vertiginous dispossession of self in the service of the other, admittedly always supposedly embodied by the widow, the orphan, and the poor, but what if the other is my executioner, my torturer, and not just mine but that of my family and friends who are still *others* among others, "those who are closest" among all those who are near to and distant from me? For the philosopher of the otherwise-than-being which is an "otherwise-than-thinking" and an "otherwise-than-loving," the responsibility that is mine extends to my responsibility for the other's wrongdoing, his or her crimes even.

For this metaphysics the word "philosophy" rediscovers its Greek root, coming from the furthest point of nonintentional consciousness. The philosopher ends his preface to the German edition of *Totality and Infinity* by asking "whether knowledge beloved of and expected from philosophers was not, beyond the wisdom of such knowledge, the wisdom of love, or wisdom in the guise of love.... A wisdom taught by the face of the other man!" (*EN* 200). But in this face-to-face, in this excessive responsibility for my neighbor, there arises too the third party, and it is at this point that the philosopher's discourse on the substitution for the other, my "uncondition as a hostage," is tempered by justice. I cannot remain indifferent to what one does to another and have to compare, judge, and consider the acts of each of my neighbors toward the other. I spoke earlier of the "asymmetry of intersubjectivity," and I am coming back to it in order to conclude, because in society I cannot be devoted just to my neighbor alone, for everyone is my neighbor. So a priority comes to light, a priority that is constitutive of the recourse to a comparative perspective, to the justice that obligates me by interrupting my one-way proximity with my neighbor in the relationships he or she has with other people. Again, in *Otherwise Than Being,* we read that "The relationship with the third party is an incessant correction of the asymmetry of proximity in which the face is looked at" (*OB* 158).

No one would deny that Levinas wanted to remind us that philosophy is the "wisdom of love," but the greatness and full scope of his philosophy is above all in his fundamental contribution to philosophy, "bringing wisdom to love" (*GCM* 110). It is by being faithful to the Jewish tradition of the Bible, through a purely philosophical and phenomenological discourse, that Levinas rediscovered the true metaphysics that comes to us from the Greeks. Levinas gave to Western philosophy an inimitable accent, a voice from elsewhere, a voice that is not just Greek, a voice that comes too from the Jewish Word, a voice that carries within it the imprescriptible tragedies of the last century, a voice that never ceased recalling that "the Place of the Good above every essence is the most profound teaching, the definitive teaching, not of theology, but of philosophy" (*TI* 103).

It is this ultimate saying of the architect of the otherwise-than-being, of the otherwise-than-thinking that is revealed in *Of God Who Comes to Mind,* which develops a new philosophical category, that of the "coming of God to mind," characterized, stigmatized almost by the suspension, the *époché*, of the "impenitent perseverance of being." This coming "of God to mind," recalls the author, cannot and "must not be taken as a 'new proof of the existence of God'" (*GCM* 168). More than ever before, we are in an exclusively philosophical domain here, one that ignores theology. Levinas did not wait for this stage in order to have recourse to the notion or concept of holiness, as if holiness ought not be of the religious domain alone but should enter on an equal footing into the field of a thought that thinks more than it thinks. We are in the metaphysical domain.

This is what Jacques Derrida heard and understood. He says so in *Adieu* with all his strength and moral authority. Let us re-read the following lines before concluding:

> Yes, ethics before and beyond ontology, the State, or politics, but also ethics beyond ethics. One day, on the rue Michel-Ange, during one of those conversations whose memory I hold so dear, one of those conversations illuminated by the radiance of his thought, the goodness of his smile, the gracious humor of his ellipses, he said to me: "You know, one often speaks of ethics to describe what I do, but what really interests me in the end is not ethics, not ethics alone, but the holy, the holiness of the holy." And I then thought of a singular separation, the unique separation of the curtain or veil that is given, ordered and ordained [*donné, ordonné*], by God, the veil entrusted by Moses to an inventor or an artist rather than to an embroiderer, the veil that would *separate* the holy of holies in the sanctuary. And I also thought of how other *Talmudic Lessons* sharpen the necessary distinction between sacredness and holiness, that is, the holiness of the other.[13]

---

13. Derrida, *Adieu to Emmanuel Levinas*, 4.

More than a tribute, these lines by Jacques Derrida express a proximity, beyond the excess, the hyperbole, the scandal almost of this "substitution." Derrida remembered the Shoah differently from Paul Ricoeur or other philosophers who never knew during the Second World War what it was to be persecuted like the Jews, or other peoples such as the Gypsies from 1944 onward and the Poles, for example.

In the very century in which the human was reduced to ashes, in which the gas chambers, the killing fields, the extermination camps, the Gulags, the atomic bomb, were all invented and destroyed tens of millions of women, men, children of all races, of all religions, as the tragic epigraph of *Otherwise Than Being or Beyond Essence* recalls, there arose a philosopher born in Lithuania, there arose a philosopher of the Jewish faith whose whole family was murdered by the Nazis. There arose a phenomenologist, a disciple of Husserl and an admirer of Heidegger's *Sein und Zeit,* a philosopher who did not forget the dimension of disinterested love when faced with the face of the other and his neighbor. There arose a philosopher for whom "the humanism of the other" prevailed over simple humanism.

> If the way that I have shown to lead to this seems to be very arduous, yet it can be discovered. And indeed it must be arduous, since it is found so rarely. For how could it happen that, if salvation were ready at hand and could be found without great labor, it is neglected by almost all? But all excellent things are as difficult as they are rare.[14]

---

14. Spinoza, *Ethics,* part 5, proposition 42 Scholium, 316.

This proposition by Spinoza, taken from the *Ethics,* applies absolutely to Levinas's work.

One last word. In the final analysis there is a remarkable nobility in this philosophy, as painful as being wrenched from oneself, like an "asymptote of the neighbor," like "a diachrony refractory to thematization"—to put it in terms of *Otherwise Than Being*—an obsession with the other taken to the point of paroxysm, with neither pathos nor rhetoric, nor too much illusion, and for which there is no greater speculation than that through which *I* am exposed and *I* reply to the often voiceless call of the person opposite me, destitute to the extreme of his or her mortal being, exhausted from moaning, exhausted from crying out. To reply to this otherwise-than-being is to be elected as the only person able to assume the choice in the name of a nontransferable responsibility: "the Messiah is Myself; to be Myself is to be the Messiah" (*DF* 89). As if all the injustice in the world, all the tragedy of the human condition were to rest on me alone and on no one else. The whole of Levinas's remarkable nobility is to have conveyed to us this expression of responsibility and suffering in a unique philosophical language, an incandescent inamissible message that can be neither lost nor forgotten, that simply expresses the dignity of the human being, of the person who in all conscience knows that he or she alone is capable of "redeem[ing] creation" (*TI* 104).

PART THREE

Forgiving and the Unforgivable in the Talmud, Based on Levinas's Teaching

1

Yom Kippur, the Day for Forgiveness

Yom Kippur and the Jewish Universality of Forgiveness

THE JEWISH YEAR RECOUNTS as it were holy history from the creation of the world commemorated in Rosh Hashanah, the New Year, to the destruction of the temple in Jerusalem on the ninth day of the month of Av (70 CE), which also marks the day of the expulsion of Spanish Jewry in 1492.

Rosh Hashanah, which precedes and announces Yom Kippur, has a universal character that no other Jewish festival has to the same degree. This festival, in all its solemnity, is the "Day of Judgment for the living." As we read at the beginning of the talmudic Tractate Rosh Hashanah (16a), "On New Year's Day all that come into the world pass before God like flocks of sheep."[1] This anniversary of the day of man's creation is also the day on which, according to tradition, Adam disobeyed God, was judged and forgiven. Beyond all religious particularism, Rosh Hashanah is meant for all human beings. From the outset, the first festival of the Jewish year bears witness to the universal theological and liturgical responsibility of Israel. The Torah does not just found the universality of Revelation, it anchors humanity's origin within it, since far from beginning with Abraham, it roots humanity in Adam, and therefore in the covenant with the Unique One. The significance of the Torah's message—beyond the people of Israel—is therefore quite simply human in that it concerns the whole of humanity. Far from having disobeyed God's word, the Jewish people were appointed its guardian; the stiff-necked people became responsible for the nations toward God.

But what sort of responsibility is at issue? The messianic responsibility of every person in Israel, in other words, the responsibility for others on account of the covenant: "You shall be to Me a kingdom of Priests and a holy nation" (Exod. 19:6). When the people of Israel, when the children of Israel will finally have heard the *Devar Adonai,* the Word of God, only then will the eyes of all people, of all tongues, of all countries, be opened and they will see Israel like a dynasty of priests, a holy nation, *ve-goy kadosh.*

Part 3 was originally published in Saint Cheron, Chalendar, and Mahfouz, *Le pardon.*

1. [This translation follows Saint Cheron's French; see also Mishnah Tractate Rosh Hashanah 1:2. The Soncino edition of the Babylonian Talmud is closer to the original Aramaic: "At New Year all creatures pass before Him [God] like children of Maron," an expression clarified by the Gemara (18a) as meaning, in Babylonian, "like a flock of sheep."—Trans.]

How does the destiny of Israel and Judaism differ from that of other religions and other peoples? It differs in that the Jewish people are destined to have a unique responsibility. A universal vocation. Just as the Merciful One forgives all Israel once a year, on Yom Kippur, so there is no redemption for Israel unless it is one. No one can be saved alone. *"Kol Ysrael yesh lahem 'helek le'olam ha'ba:* All Israel have a portion in the world to come," as it is written in the Tractate Sanhedrin (90a). We have no solitary salvation. Which is why it is only when our responsibility has become universal, extended to all Israel and to all peoples, that we will really have understood Moses' words: "For this commandment that I command you today—it is not hidden from you and it is not distant. It is not in heaven.... Nor is it across the sea.... Rather, the matter is very near to you—in your mouth and your heart—to perform it" (Deut. 30:11–14).

It is in the human heart and uniquely there that the Torah lives, the Word of God as he revealed it to humanity, and first to Israel. But to hear this voice, one first needs to listen to it. This is why every observant Jew recites *"Shema Ysrael,* Hear, O Israel" three times a day. The liturgy of Rosh Hashanah teaches us that on this anniversary of the day the world was created, all humankind is summoned before God's court:

> The great *shofar* will be sounded and a still, thin sound will be heard. Angels will hasten, a trembling and terror will seize them.... All mankind will pass before You like members of the flock. Like a shepherd pasturing his flock, making sheep consider the soul of all the living; and You shall apportion the fixed needs of all Your creatures and inscribe their verdict.[2]

---

2. *ArtScroll Machzor Rosh Hashanah,* 479.

If Rosh Hashanah is the Day of Judgment for the nations, does it follow that Yom Kippur is the Day of Forgiveness for all mankind? No doubt Yom Kippur does have a universal dimension, which is why our sages insisted on introducing into the liturgy of Kippur the reading of the book of Jonah, the prophet who went off to convert the inhabitants of Nineveh and their king.[3] But this reading of Jonah nevertheless remains a lesson specifically for Jews on this day of repentance and expiation, about their spiritual role and their nontransferable responsibility toward the whole of humankind, even if it is conceivably a means of extending divine forgiveness to all the Just of the nations. Immediately after the third repetition by the cantor and the congregation of *Kol Nidrei,* the eponymous prayer of Kippur's evening service, does the cantor not recite, repeated by the chorus of the faithful, the following verse from Numbers (15:26): "May it be forgiven for the entire congregation of the Children of Israel and for the stranger who dwells among them, for [the sin] befell the entire nation through carelessness."[4]

THE PRAYER SERVICE FOR KIPPUR

In the book of Leviticus (23:27–29), we read: "But on the tenth day of this month it is the Day of Atonement (*Yom haKippurim*); there shall be a holy convocation for you, and you shall afflict yourselves; you shall offer a fire-offering to HaShem. You shall not do any work on this very day, for it is the Day of Atonement (*Yom Kippurim*)

---

3. [To be precise, God calls upon Jonah to warn the people of Nineveh that if they do not repent they will be destroyed; the biblical text does not expressly speak of conversion. —Trans.]

4. *ArtScroll Machzor Yom Kippur,* 69.

to provide you atonement before HaShem, your God." An absolute abstention from work and a fast characterize the Day of Atonement, also called Yom Kippur, the Day of Forgiveness. Only in Judaism is there a day of forgiveness, a fact that immediately raises questions. So what is Yom Kippur? The holiest day of the Jewish year, exclusively devoted to making amends for one's transgressions, to their expiation through a total fast, accompanied by numerous forms of abstinence from sunset of the preceding day to sundown of the day itself. During these 25 hours of fasting, as if freed from one's daily needs—so many obstacles to the true freedom of mind and body—the Jew himself or herself becomes prayer.

On the eve of Yom Kippur, three men begin the *Kol Nidrei* service with this curious prayer: "With the approval of the Omnipresent and with the approval of the congregation; in the convocation of the Court above and in the convocation of the Court below, we sanction prayer with the transgressors."[5] What does this preliminary declaration signify? One might think that our holy sages were inspired to include this permission to pray with the transgressors by the tragic period of the Inquisition when the "marranos" (those who were forcibly converted) came to pray in secret, but also by the multitude of the "Jews of Kippur" who are Jews for one day a year. Of all the solemn rituals of the Jewish year, not one speaks to Jews from so deeply within, whether as a community or as individuals. To see the multitude of Jews hurrying to the synagogues on Yom Kippur Eve, just as they will do the following evening for the closing service we call

---

5. Ibid., 67. [Most customs have only the cantor, or one of the two men flanking him, declare this part of the *Kol Nidrei* prayer.—Trans.]

Neilah, we feel a mixture of happiness and emotion, but also pride in seeing our brothers and sisters respond in this way to the holy convocation decreed more than 3,000 years ago in the Sinai desert by the God of Israel and of all peoples, in words related by Moses our master.

That forgiveness in Judaism should be fixed once and for all by a calendar gives it unique strength. That it cannot take place on just any day, but on this day "second to none" called Yom Kippur, gives the ritual, the *tchouvah,* the "return" consecrated by this ritual, an incomparable uniqueness that transports soul and body, and lifts Jewish women and men to heights that cannot be attained alone, unless one is carried on the wings of the *Shekhinah,* the Presence of God that accompanies Israel in its exile. That the Holy One, blessed be He should have given Yom Kippur to the Jewish people, a day that is renewed only once a year, must help us to realize that forgiveness is something holy; it needs this temporal mark, this absolute separation with the temporality of time, the everyday that wears out all it touches in order to remind us that it runs the risk at any moment of being cut off from its holiness.

Separation, holiness, but also specificity. For Jewish forgiveness cannot be reduced to any of its equivalents. In French as in German, the word "pardon" [forgiveness] seems to have a relation with the gift [*don,* what is *given*], but in Hebrew the word *kappara* comes from the root *kappar,* which means "to cover." Jewish forgiveness, then, has nothing of a gift about it, but everything of a reparation, a recovering, a recuperation even, an expiation. The three consonants of the root *kappar* also give *kipper,* which means "to appease," "to absolve," "to erase an error." Resorting to the etymology of the word "forgiveness" in Hebrew is not of secondary importance; it shows how much a word reveals a thought, an irreducible world vision. Let us go further into the difference between the Jewish and French meaning of the word "pardon" [forgiveness]. One can receive a gift [*don,* donation] without effort, without asking even, or without expectations, but one cannot be cleansed of one's transgressions without having worked toward effectively expiating them—a personal spiritual effort—nor can one obtain reparation without repairing anything oneself.

This Jewish experience of forgiveness shows a considerable awareness of man's place in Judaism. In Israel's long history, numerous Jews, impervious to all forms of ritual or liturgy, have rediscovered their deep-rootedness on Yom Kippur. The revelation that some of these Jews have been able to have one Yom Kippur evening is incomparable, because it is not just a personal experience but more like a resurrection in the heart of Israel's community. To regain one's Jewishness at Kippur is a little like entering Judaism through the gate of forgiveness. The great philosopher Franz Rosenzweig experienced this *tchouvah,* this reversal of being, at the beginning of the century on the eve of a conversion to Christianity, which then became impossible. One might say that the *kappara,* the forgiveness that was at work then was inamissible, which in the theological sense of the term means that it cannot be lost.

But to know the Jewish vision of forgiveness uniquely through the words of the Kippur ritual is to know nothing about it at all. Faced with someone who has been offended, a victim of his or her neighbor, God, the Judge, who at the same time is the Merciful One, by totally erasing himself in an act of *tsimtsoum,* does not substitute himself for the victim in order to forgive the assailant. The liturgy of Yom Kippur, the holy of holies, can do nothing if I have not succeeded in obtaining forgiveness from the person I have offended.

Let's enter the day's liturgy and reveal its high points. What is so striking at first is the brilliant whiteness that adorns the synagogue on this day, from the curtain decorating the cabinet in which the scrolls of the Torah are stored, to the mats covering the seats for the members of the community. Jews who are particularly observant don the *sargueness* [or *kittel*], the mortuary costume which recalls both the day of death and the High Priest dressed in white linen when he would pronounce the ineffable Name on Kippur in the temple in Jerusalem. Everyone is also wrapped in the white *tallith,* the prayer shawl worn by men in the mornings at synagogue. Everything is ready for the service to begin, a service that from evening to evening lasts no less than twelve hours: two hours in the evening and almost ten hours the day itself. The Kippur ritual is extremely simple, very few movements, a few chants repeated several times like a dialogue between the cantor and the faithful. Like entreaties they allow the lamentations and wailing of the suffering soul to be heard as they rise toward Adonai full of mercy and love for his repentant children.

The liturgy of atonement is notable for the desire the lawmakers of Israel had for every Jew—for everyone in Israel—to feel both responsible and guilty on their own account and on account of the others; responsible for the sins committed by myself—or not, but which I could have committed—responsible for my Jewish brother, as it is written: "All Israel are sureties one for another" (talmudic Tractate Shebuoth 39a)—and for all humankind.[6] This

---

6. [This is Saint Cheron's reading of the Gemara—consistent with Levinas's own humanist optic; as the Soncino edition notes,

is why several times during this day we recite the *Viduy,* the Confession of Sins. Without this confession there can be no forgiveness. We painfully chant these words whose translation renders nothing of the voiceless trembling that accompanies them:

Ashamnu, bagadnu, gazalnu, dibarnu dofi. He'evinu, vehirshanu, zadnu, 'hamasnu, tafalnu sheker.... We have become guilty, we have betrayed, we have robbed, we have spoken slander. We have caused perversion, we have caused wickedness, we have sinned willfully, we have extorted, we have accused falsely. We have counseled evil, we have been deceitful, we have scorned, we have rebelled, we have provoked, we have turned away, we have been perverse, we have acted wantonly, we have persecuted, we have been obstinate. We have been wicked, we have corrupted, we have been abominable, we have strayed, You let us go astray.[7]

There follows a long prayer which begins with these words: "And so may it be Your will, HaShem, our God and the God of our forefathers, that You atone for us and for all our errors, and You forgive us for all our iniquities, and You pardon us for all our willful sins."[8]

"The celebration of *Yom Kippur* and the spiritual state it brings about or expresses lead us to the state of forgiven beings" (*NT* 16), writes Emmanuel Levinas, adding that this method holds only for the faults committed against God. But the forgiveness is not brought about by

---

the "whole world" in the Gemara here means the "whole world of Israel": "Hence, in the case of all transgressions the whole world (of Israel) is punished, because all Israelites are responsible for one another, and bound to prevent wrongdoing!"—Trans.]
7. *ArtScroll Machzor Yom Kippur,* 25.
8. Ibid., 25.

a miracle, one has to repent with *kavanah,* intention in Hebrew. Repentance without intention is nothing, just as forgiveness without expiation is inconceivable. On Rosh Hashanah as on Kippur we say the following fearsome prayer but one that opens onto humankind's laborious hope:

> On Rosh Hashanah will be inscribed and on Yom Kippur will be sealed how many will pass from the earth and how many will be created; who will live and who will die; who will die at his predestined time and who before his time; who by water and who by fire, who by sword, who by beast, who by famine, who by thirst, who by storm, who by plague, who by strangulation, and who by stoning. Who will rest and who will wander, who will live in harmony and who will be harried, who will enjoy tranquillity [sic] and who will suffer, who will be impoverished and who will be enriched, who will be degraded and who will be exalted. But *repentance, prayer* and *charity* remove the evil of the decree! For Your Name signifies Your praise: hard to anger and easy to appease, for You do not wish the death of one deserving death, but that he repent from his way and live. Until the day of his death You await him; if he repents You will accept him immediately.[9]

Tchouvah, tefillah, and *zdakah* (repentance, prayer, charity) are the most powerful arms in the hands of the sinner. They alone bring forgiveness on Kippur. They are inseparable and their indissolubility alone testifies to the *kavanah,* the repentant's spiritual intention. Not that everything is resolved, for the *tchouvah, tefillah,* and *zdakah* say nothing of the sins committed against another person. Indeed, whereas in order to repent I am

---

9. *ArtScroll Machzor Rosh Hashanah,* 479, 481.

alone with myself—and with God—in order to receive the other's forgiveness one has to be at least two, the other and myself, and three with HaShem.

The Torah teaches us that intercession is one of the first methods of forgiveness. Abraham's extraordinary intercession in favor of Sodom is the very example to instruct us. Forgiveness through intercession—practically nonexistent today—teaches us that it depends both on the person or persons for whom one is interceding, and on the person who takes upon himself or herself the sins of others. For if Abraham in his bargaining with the Most High had come down to just one righteous person to save Sodom, who knows if it would not have been saved! But, conversely, if there had been but ten righteous people, it would not have been destroyed. Is this also not taking into account the children who even in Sodom had to have been innocent? Moses as Israel's shepherd after the collective sin of the Golden Calf interceded with Israel's Holy One and won out by imploring for all of Israel. Forgiveness for the Jew is inseparable from the forgiveness granted *Klal Ysrael,* all of Israel, as is forcefully apparent in the Kippur liturgy. What prevails here is not the search for salvation or for individual forgiveness but the desire for the atonement—and Redemption—of all the people of Israel. When it implores forgiveness from the Holy One, blessed be He, Israel is undivided.

I would like to relate a teaching of one of the finest figures of European Jewish orthodoxy, the Tzadik Rabbi Hayyim Yaakov Rottenberg, of blessed memory, who from 1964 to his death three weeks before Rosh Hashanah 5751 (August 1990), was the chief rabbi of the orthodox community of Paris in the rue Pavé. "As long as the Jew feels he belongs to the people of Israel, all is still possible," he used to say. "Sins can be forgiven if he feels he belongs to the collectivity." And he would add, in a commentary on the famous words in the Tractate Sanhedrin (90a): "*Kol Ysrael*... All Israel have a portion in the world to come": "It does not say all 'Jews,' but all 'Israel,' to teach us that this is only valid if one feels one belongs to the people of Israel." Rabbi Rottenberg's words carry within them an age-old teaching on which the survival of the Jewish people rests. A Jew who abandons the Torah, but above all who abandons his people, is deprived at the same time of God's pardon for all of Israel.

In the temple era, the High Priest would intercede on Yom Kippur for all Israel. It is about him that Leviticus 16:17 says, "he shall provide atonement for himself, for his household, and for the entire congregation of Israel." The additional service on the morning of Kippur, *Mussaf*, is the memorial of the service performed on that day by the High Priest, the *Kohen Gadol*. Particular mention is made of the ceremony of the two he-goats picked by lots, offered by the congregation of Israel and intended to "bring atonement upon the Children of Israel for all their sins" (Lev. 16:34). One of the he-goats was designated for the altar, in other words for God, the other had to symbolically bear all the iniquities of Israel and was sent to the wilderness where it was thrown into the void "so that as it fell into the abyss" it took with it "all traces of iniquity from the people." This he-goat was designated the scapegoat, but the modern meaning given to this expression is totally distorted. The scapegoat for Kippur was not an animal to be cast out, responsible for everyone's ills; on the contrary, it was pure of all blemish and still served to wash Israel of its sins. The other he-goat symbolized the holiest part of the Jewish people, designated to be lifted up toward the Holy One, blessed be He, as a propitiatory sacrifice.

"Now that the *Beit Hamikdash* [temple] is no more, and we have neither Cohen [priest] nor altar, nor offerings for atonement, we recite the order of the *avodah* [the Yom Kippur temple service]."[10] Faced with the destruction of the temple, our sages, of blessed memory, prescribed the practice of reciting during the repetition of the *Mussaf* service the entire service by the High Priest as it took place on Yom Kippur. As Hosea (14:3) says, "let our lips substitute for bulls."

As this day of atonement draws to a close, during the final *Neilah* prayer, just when the doors are closing on the holy cabinet containing the Torah scrolls, God forgives his children assembled together for the sins committed against him. The extreme tension that has been mounting up since the previous evening explodes in the *Shema Ysrael* prayer, as in the final *Avinu Malkeinu,* Our Father, our King, chanted by the entire congregation just after the priestly blessing of the *kohanim,* the descendants of the priests, who go up next to the altar, cover their head with their *tallith,* their prayer shawl, and begin the solemn cantillation. The *Neilah* closes with the blowing of the *shofar,* which marks the end of Kippur, at the same time as the distancing of the divine Presence, as it is written in Psalms 47:6: "God has ascended with the blast [*terouah*]; HaShem, with the sound of the *shofar.*"[11]

---

10. Kitov, *The Book of Our Heritage,* 1:121.
11. The word *terouah* means sigh, sob, weeping, all symbolized by the blast of the *shofar,* the ram's horn symbolizing the ram offered up by Abraham instead of Isaac on Mount Moriah.

THE ATONEMENT OF SINS AGAINST GOD

Let us now look at the sins committed by humanity against God. We need to go back to the original sin before opening the Talmud. For Adam and Eve's sin is definitely a sin against God—moreover, it is the only original meaning given to it by rabbinical and talmudic tradition, which never saw a hereditary sin in it. What is more, as we have seen, Adam was judged on Rosh Hashanah, repented, and the Holy One, blessed be He, forgave him: "You are a sign unto your children; as you were judged before me this day and emerged forgiven, so will your children be judged before me this day, and emerge forgiven."[12] One might equally imagine a sage protesting against the very notion of original sin and saying, like Kafka: "Original sin, the old injustice committed by man, consists in man's reproach—which he cannot relinquish—that he has been done an injustice, that an original sin was committed against him."[13]

How can one speak of forgiveness in Judaism without first raising the unavoidable question as to why the God of Israel has been seen for so long as a cruel God, vengeful, pitiless and unjust? This is so because the text of the Torah has long been read *literally,* often in ignorance of tradition and commentary—starting with Rashi, the brilliant French Jewish exegete of the Middle Ages—commentary that is inseparable from the verse in the Torah it is commenting upon. Let us take an example that is as striking as it is apparently unjust and pitiless. It comes

---

12. *Pesikta de Rav Kahana,* cited by Kitov, *The Book of Our Heritage,* 1:20.
13. [Translated from Kafka, *Oeuvres complètes* 3:496. This diary entry, dated January–February 1920, does not appear in the English translation of the *Diaries of Franz Kafka.* —Trans.]

from the end of Exodus 34:7: "[God recalls] the iniquity of parents upon children and grandchildren, to the third and fourth generations." What does Rashi have to say about this famous verse that has been the object of the most contrary interpretations to Jewish tradition?

> He clears [forgives] those who repent but does not clear those who will not repent. *Visiting the iniquity of the fathers upon the children*—when they retain in their hands (follow the example of) the evil doings of their ancestors. This must be the meaning because in another verse *of a similar character* it has already been stated: "of them that hate Me" (Exod. 20:5).... *And upon the fourth generation.* It follows, therefore, that the measure of good (reward) is greater than the measure of punishment in the proportion of one to five hundred, for in respect to the measure of good it says: "keeping mercy for thousands" (two thousands at least).[14]

We are far from a vengeful, pitiless, unjust God!

To speak of forgiveness is necessarily to speak of sin, of evil, which is why it was important to specify the Jewish conception of the relation between sin and collective guilt. For Judaism, the entire ethical urgency emerges more from Cain's original crime than from Adam and Eve's sin, because in the latter case all three protagonists are guilty together for disobeying God's word, whereas in the episode of the primordial murder, the drama is played out between a murderer and an innocent person, and, what is more, between two brothers.

It is now time to open the Talmud to Tractate Yoma 85b and read the Mishnah:

---

14. *Chumash,* vol. 2, *Shemoth,* 192–93.

The Sin-offering and the Guilt-offering [for the] undoubted commission of certain offences, procure atonement, death and the Day of Atonement procure atonement together with penitence. Penitence procures atonement for lighter transgressions: [the transgressions of] positive commandments and prohibitions. In the case of severer transgressions it [penitence] suspends [the divine punishment] until the Day of Atonement comes to procure atonement. If one says, "I shall sin and repent, sin and repent," no opportunity will be given to him to repent. [If one says,] "I shall sin and the Day of Atonement will procure atonement for me," the Day of Atonement procures for him no atonement. For transgressions as between man and the Omnipresent, the Day of Atonement procures atonement, but for transgressions as between man and his fellow the Day of Atonement does not procure any atonement, until he has pacified his fellow. This was expounded by R. Eleazar b. Azariah: *From all your sins before the Lord shall ye be clean* (Lev. 16:30)—for transgressions as between man and the Omnipresent the Day of Atonement procures atonement, but for transgressions as between man and his fellow the Day of Atonement does not procure atonement until he has pacified his fellow. R. Akiba said: Happy are you, Israel! Who is it before whom you become clean? And who is it that makes you clean? Your Father which is in heaven, as it is said, *And I will sprinkle clean water upon you and ye shall be clean* (Ezek. 36:25). And it further says, *Thou hope* (mikveh) *of Israel, the Lord!* (Jer. 17:13). Just as the fountain [*mikveh*] renders clean the unclean, so does the Holy One, blessed be He, render clean Israel.[15]

---

15. [For an alternative translation, see Mishnah, Tractate Yoma 8:8–9.—Trans.]

This is one of the Talmud's founding texts on forgiveness. It is not the only one, far from it. It is, however, one of the most remarkable for the range of questions it raises. It is this very page (though abridged) from the Tractate Yoma that Emmanuel Levinas commented upon nearly 50 years ago in the context of the colloquium of Jewish intellectuals devoted to "Forgiveness."[16]

Let's come back to our Mishnah: death or the day of Kippur procures atonement.... A curious connection or parallelism between death, characterized in the Jewish tradition by impurity, and Yom Kippur, the holiest day of the year, as if death and Kippur were equivalent and had the same power to atone. If death procures the atonement of transgressions, are we to understand that it procures atonement for all transgressions or just the transgressions committed against God? It can only concern the transgressions committed against him, since we have been taught that "the grave will [not] be thy refuge."[17]

Our Mishnah goes further: death itself atones for nothing without repentance. If repentance alone obtains atonement for the transgressions of positive or negative commandments—transgressions, therefore, that can be atoned for—for what transgressions can death, relieved by repentance, obtain atonement? Is it not for the severest transgressions committed against the Holy One, blessed be He—with the exception of those committed against others? And can we not ask, following on from our *Baraitha*,[18] what the transgressions are for which repentance suspends punishment?

---

16. [See "Toward the Other" in *NT* 12–29.—Trans.]
17. Mishnah, Tractate Aboth [Ethics of the Fathers], 4:22.
18. An Aramaic word meaning "outside" and designating the parts omitted by the Mishnah.

Are the transgressions that carry the death penalty by a rabbinical court (*beth din*) not atoned for by natural death, preceded by repentance? Our Gemara (86a) provides us with the beginning of an answer:

> But if he has been guilty of the profanation of the Name [of God], then penitence has no power to suspend punishment, nor the Day of Atonement to procure atonement, nor suffering to finish it, but all of them together [penitence, Kippur, suffering] suspend the punishment and only death finishes it, as it is said: "And the Lord of hosts revealed Himself in my ears; surely this iniquity shall not be expiated by you till ye die" (Isa. 22:14).

But today when rabbinical courts no longer have jurisprudence over life, what is substituted for sacrifice and atonement, in place of what was customary during the temple period? It is the great Lithuanian talmudist Rabbi Hayyim Volozhiner, a disciple of the Gaon of Vilna, who enlightens us through his erudition and wisdom:

> A man who has committed numerous transgressions and has been judged guilty of death (by God)..., if he repents, studies Torah, the Prophets, the Hagiographies, the Mishnah, the Midrash, the Halakhot, the Aggadot, places himself in the service of the *Hakhamim* (the Sages) of the Torah—were he to be condemned a hundred times, God annuls all punishment.

A passage from the Talmud (Tractate Rosh Hashanah 18a) clarifies this:

> The study of Torah brings forgiveness even for the grave transgressions that sacrifices do not atone for, as our masters point out concerning the sons of Eli: "Therefore I have sworn concerning the house of Eli that the son of the house of Eli would never be atoned for by sacrifice or meal-offering" (1 Sam. 3:14)—The

sin cannot be atoned for by sacrifice or meal-offering, but it can be atoned for by the study of Torah.[19]

Judaism has never preached for latecomers; on the contrary, it has taught without respite that there is more merit in obeying what has been commanded than in accomplishing what has not been commanded. In his commentary on Leviticus 26:9, Rashi relates the following magnificent Midrash:

> A king had many laborers. One laborer was there who had done work for the king many days. When they were to receive their wages the king said to him: "My son, I must turn my attention specially to you—let me first reward these here who have done little work and the paying off of whom will not take me long. With you, however, I have to settle large accounts, and this I wish to do at leisure."[20]

Two readings initially present themselves; the first, following the literal meaning, called the *pshat* in the Hebrew terminology, reinforces the idea that the perfectly righteous person has more merit than those who became righteous late in life, for steadfastness, the daily effort to remain faithful to the Torah, is incontestably and infinitely more difficult than the fidelity found in the exaltation of becoming religious. The second reading, following the symbolic meaning, the *drash,* implies that the most faithful and also the oldest worker is none other than Israel, who was the first to hear and accept the Revelation.

---

19. [Although Rabbi Hayyim Volozhiner's classic commentary on Pirkei Avoth (Ethics of the Fathers) has recently been translated into English, there is, surprisingly, no English translation of his *Nefesh HaHayyim* (The Soul of Life); the translation here therefore follows the French translation in Hayyim de Volozhyn, *L'âme de la vie,* 240–41.—Trans.]
20. See *Chumash,* vol. 3, *Vayikra,* 199.

2

Our Transgressions against Our Fellows

THE ORIGINAL MURDER AND VENGEANCE

AFTER CAIN'S MURDER OF ABEL his brother, he heard a divine voice asking him, "Where is Abel your brother?" Cain replied: "I do not know. Am I my brother's keeper?" HaShem then said: "What have you done? The voice of your brother's blood cries out to Me from the ground!" (Gen. 4:9–10).

Abel is dead, but what has not died with him is the voice of his blood, or more exactly of *his bloods, kol demei,* which needs to be understood as Rashi does: his blood and the blood of his descendents. This recalls the famous talmudic saying, "whosoever destroys a single soul of Israel, Scripture imputes [guilt] to him as though he had destroyed a complete world; and whosoever preserves a single soul of Israel, Scripture ascribes [merit] to him as though he had preserved a complete world"

(Sanhedrin 37a).[1] What is the voice of blood if not the human soul? Cain had no inkling of just how much he was his brother's keeper. Was it for lack of hearing the *Lo tirtzakh,* the "Thou shalt not kill," that Cain killed Abel? Or for not having accepted that the Holy One, blessed be He, could prefer his brother's offering to his own?

Remorse does not seem to have opened a flaw in his conscience. The Midrash recounts that when HaShem asked Cain, "Where is Abel your brother?," Cain replied, "I killed him. You created in me an evil impulse. You watch over everything, and yet You allowed me to kill him. It is You who killed him, for You are called 'I.'"[2]

This text places the entire responsibility for evil on God. One may object that that is the price (though in truth an exorbitant one) of human freedom. But the greatness of the God of Israel is to have created a man capable not only of refuting him but also of indicting him. That such liberty is absolutely inadmissible in Islam is what opens the door to the radical fanaticism of so many of its followers. The fact remains that this liberty demonstrates the specificity of the relations between the children of Israel and their God. Relations that can be understood if one sees in them proof of Israel's primogeniture.

And yet to hold God responsible for all the evil within us—not to mention the evil whose absolute symbol is the Shoah—considerably reduces human beings to nothing

---

1. Maimonides gives a universal meaning to the teaching contained in the talmudic adage: "Therefore man was created alone in the world in order to teach that if one destroys a single human life, Scripture sees him as if he destroyed the entire world; and if one saves a single human life, Scripture sees him as if he saved the entire world."
2. [See Midrash Tanchuma, *Bereishis* 1:9, 54.—Trans.]

but puppets. This simplistic conception of evil and our powerlessness to face up to it are at the very least radically opposed to the teaching of the Torah whereby we must choose between good and evil, between life and death. Cain suddenly becomes aware of his sin when he says: "*Gadol avoni minso,* My iniquity [is] too great to be borne" (Gen. 4:13), which Rashi understands as a question: "You bear the worlds above and below, and is it impossible for You to bear my sin?" In saying *Godol avoni minso,* did Cain not want to say in effect, "Is my iniquity unforgivable?"

If Adonai, the God of mercy,[3] were to bear the sin, he would forgive it. But does he bear it? If the text of the Torah is to be believed, the reply is negative: "Therefore, you are cursed more than the ground, which opened wide its mouth to receive your brother's blood from your hand. When you work the ground, it shall no longer yield its strength to you. You shall become a vagrant and a wanderer on earth" (Gen. 4:11–12). Because this passage goes to the heart of the problem of evil and conscience, we understand why the question of sin and responsibility is so deeply rooted in it. If Adam and Eve's sin against God alone was forgiven, Cain's crime, committed against the person of his brother, could only have been forgiven by the victim, and tradition has not taught that the dead Abel forgave.

Neither vengeance nor forgiveness by proxy can redeem the death of a human being. Only a free and totally human justice has any legitimate place. But our sages repeatedly said that on a strictly personal level

---

3. [Saint Cheron writes "le Dieu matriciel," again referring to the Hebrew word for mercy, *rahamim,* and its root *rehem,* meaning womb; see above, p. 5.— Trans.]

vengeance is opposed to forgiveness. Hence in the Tractate Megillah 28a, Raba says, "He who waives his right to retribution is forgiven all his sins, as it says: '[God] pardoneth iniquity and passeth by transgression' (Micah 7:18). Whose iniquity is forgiven? The iniquity of him who passes by transgression." Here is a problematic passage from 2 Samuel 21:1–9 which is clarified and commented on in the talmudic Tractate Yebamoth (79a) and to which Emmanuel Levinas once devoted an admirable commentary.[4] David is looking to atone for the crime committed by Saul against the Gibeonites. He says to them, "What can I do for you, and how can I atone [for this sin], so that you will bless the heritage of HaShem?," adding, "Whatever you say I will do for you." They reply to the king, "The man who annihilated us and who schemed against us that we be eliminated from remaining within the entire border of Israel—let seven men of his sons be given to us and we will hang them for the sake of HaShem in the Gibeah of Saul (the chosen one of HaShem)." David delivered them to the Gibeonites but spared Mephibosheth, the son of Jonathan and Saul's grandson. "They hanged them on the mountain before Hashem; all seven of them fell together."

What does this text mean? Is it not written: "Fathers shall not be put to death because of sons, and sons shall not be put to death because of fathers" (Deut. 24:16)? Rabbi Hiyya b. Abba said, in the name of Rabbi Johanan, "It is better that a letter be rooted out of the Torah than that the Divine Name shall be publicly profaned" (Yebamoth 79a). How should David's refusal to hand over

---

4. [In "Toward the Other," where the page in Tractate Yebamoth is mistakenly referenced as 58b–59a; see *NT* 25–28.—Trans.]

seven of Saul's sons to be hanged because of the crimes of their father have been understood as a profanation of the divine Name? Was this act of vengeance, which was made possible for the Gibeonites by David, the best way to bless HaShem's heritage? Did he accept this blessing? This does not seem to be what preoccupied the *Hakhamim,* the talmudic sages. They turn the problematic around: if the Gibeonites, who in all likelihood had never heard the Ten Commandments from Sinai and in particular "Thou shalt not kill," had not acted in this way, then their deaths would have gone unpunished. As if for our sages the fact that murder cannot go unpunished were to prevail over the profanation of the divine Name! This commentary that sounds so terrible to our modern ears signifies that in order for the crime against the stranger not to go unpunished in Eretz Israel, the land of Israel, the king of Israel could go so far as to contravene a verse from the Torah.

During the temple period, only the Sanhedrin, the supreme court consisting of 23 or 71 members, could condemn someone to death, on condition, however, that there were two witnesses to the crime and that they had had time to warn the assailant of the penalty. The Tractate Makkoth (7a) teaches that "a Sanhedrin that effects an execution once in seven years is branded a destructive tribunal; R. Eleazar b. Azariah says: Once in seventy years. R. Tarfon and R. Akiba say: Were we members of a Sanhedrin, no person would be put to death."[5] In the modern State of Israel, the death sentence was never instituted. An exceptional arrangement allowed Adolf Eichmann to be condemned to death.

---

5. [See also Mishnah, Tractate Makkoth 1:10.—Trans.]

THE MODALITIES OF FORGIVENESS

> For transgressions as between man and the Omnipresent the Day of Atonement procures atonement, but for transgressions as between man and his fellow the Day of Atonement does not procure any atonement, until he has pacified his fellow...
>
> It is for the transgressions of man against God that the Day of Atonement procures forgiveness, but for the transgressions of man against another person, the Day of Atonement procures forgiveness only if he has obtained forgiveness from his fellow.[6]

The last lines of this fundamental passage for the Jewish teaching of forgiveness are in fact a commentary by Rabbi Eleazar ben Azariah of the verse in Leviticus (16:30): "from all your sins before HaShem shall you be cleansed." In a Christian civilization—or in any case a civilization with Christian values such as our own—but not one that is *Judeo*-Christian, this text provides ground for surprise since it contradicts all preconceived ideas on forgiveness.

In these lines from the Tractate Yoma (85b), God does not substitute himself for the victim in order to forgive the guilty party. Some might infer from this that it is because God is indifferent. On the contrary, every crime committed by one person against another is a crime before God. In the Jewish tradition, God's true enemies have always been the enemies of Israel, which one can well understand. Two surprisingly audacious remarks are called for here. On the one hand, the creator of the world is powerless

---

6. [Talmudic Tractate Yoma 85b, following in the first instance the translation of the Soncino edition. Saint Cheron first gives Levinas's translation of this passage, reproduced in English in *NT* 12 (and erroneously attributed to Yoma 85a), and follows it with his own translation, which I translate here accordingly.—Trans.]

to forgive the transgressions committed by one person against another! On the other hand, the forgiveness of our transgressions against others cannot tolerate either human or divine proxy. God can do nothing to make up for one person's crime against another. The transcendence of forgiveness can be accomplished only in the immanence of sociality. God's supreme humility!

The Holy One, blessed be He, grants us, therefore, the power to forgive what neither the sin offering (in Hebrew *kaporet*, a word with the same root as *kippur* and *kappara*, as we have seen previously) of long ago nor Yom Kippur itself can forgive. When the Midrash declares that the Ark of the Covenant (the Holy of Holies from Moses to the temple in Jerusalem) "brings forgiveness to Israel,"[7] it is speaking only of the people's transgressions committed against God. A decisive Gemara further on in Tractate Yoma (87a) objects that the transgressions by one man against another cannot be forgiven by Yom Kippur: "R. Joseph b. Helbe pointed out to R. Abbahu the following contradiction: [we learned]: 'for transgressions committed by man against his fellowman the day of atonement procures no atonement,' but it is written: 'If one man sin against his fellow-man, God [*Elohim*] will pacify him' (1 Sam. 2:25)."

God is referred to here by the word *Elohim*, the judge. "But if a man sin against the Lord, who shall entreat for

---

7. See Midrash Tanchuma, *Shemos*, vol. 2, *Vayakhel* 7–10; cited in Hayyim de Volozhyn, *L'âme de la vie*, 240. [In fact, the Midrash Tanchuma does not say that the Ark of the Covenant as such procures atonement but rather the *seraphim*, the angels that were placed on it ("for they were the atonement," 371) and the *kaporet*, the Ark cover ("through the Arkcover I will forgive you," 388). — Trans.]

him?" And this is Rabbi Abbahu's reply: "If a man sins against his fellow-man, the judge will judge him, he [his fellow] will forgive him; but if a man sins against the Lord God, who shall entreat for him? Only repentance and good deeds."

Is this not irrefutable proof that neither good deeds nor repentance can provide forgiveness where "man is concerned"? *Tchouvah* (repentance), *tefilah* (prayer), and *zdakah* (charity), which are all-powerful to annul the fatal decree between Rosh Hashanah and Yom Kippur, can do nothing, therefore, if the person who has been offended through my sin has not forgiven me. What happens if I wanted to obtain his forgiveness but he refuses to grant it? R. Jose b. Hanina replies (87a), "One who asks pardon of his neighbour need not do so more than three times." His reply is based on the prayer of Joseph's brothers after the death of their father Jacob: "O please, kindly forgive..., so now, please forgive" (Gen. 50:17).[8]

But another question immediately arises, an even graver one: what if the person (meanwhile) has died? "[The guilty party] should bring ten persons and make them stand by his grave and say: I have sinned against the Lord [*Elohim*], the God of Israel, and against this one, whom I have hurt" (87a). But what about the murderer? Is forgiveness even possible, given the impossibility for the dead person to forgive postmortem and the impossibility for anyone at all to forgive in place of the person who is no longer with us? In the very mysterious chapter in Deuteronomy (21:1–8), it is written, "If a corpse will be found on the land that HaShem, your God, gives you to

---

8. [In Hebrew it is the term *na* (O, pray) that is used three times. — Trans.]

possess it, fallen in the field, it was not known who smote him," then the elders and judges of the city nearest the corpse have to make a guilt-offering with a heifer, pronouncing the following words over it: "Our hands have not spilled this blood, and our eyes did not see. Atone for Your people Israel that You have redeemed, O HaShem: Do not place innocent blood in the midst of Your people Israel!"

In this context, in what way is Eichmann's sentence by the Jerusalem Court—ratified by the Supreme Court of Israel and the Jerusalem Court of Appeal—truly exceptional in the context of Israeli justice inherited from the Torah and Talmud? It is exceptional precisely because of a talmudic ruling related to the Sanhedrin—which would be worth pausing over at great length—according to which a death sentence unanimously pronounced by its 23 members must not be executed and entails quite to the contrary the obligation to acquit the accused. How is it that a unanimous death sentence not *can* be but *must* be contested? It is the unanimity that has to be questioned, because if all the judges decide on capital punishment then mercy has not been heard in the midst of the Sanhedrin. There must always be in the midst of harsh but righteous judges, a disciple of Rabbi Akiba or Rabbi Tarfon, to be the advocate for the God of forgiveness, to be the advocate for mercy. It is only on this condition that the judges' majority can win out, so that strict justice can be applied. Eichmann, however, could not fall under any jurisdiction that would have followed these general rules, given the exceptional—to say the least!—character of his inamissible crimes, which did not stop his first sentence from being referred to the Court of Appeal. But let us come back to the ordinary context, to which the talmudic interdiction applies, and in particular to Rashi's commentary: "If what is said about the man—as it happens, a man accused of a crime punishable by death—is identical to the idea one has of him, then there is no longer any justice."[9] An admirable thought indeed which would have justice possible only if there is no correlation between what is said and being judged objectively and the subjectivity of the judges.

In a world in which forgiveness is possible whenever we want it, does it not risk being devalued? For there is the suffering of the other, the suffering of all others, which no forgiveness will relieve. What forgiveness is there when faced with my crimeless but infinite guilt? Is there a guilt, however, which is beyond the scope of forgiveness, which exceeds it? Does a form of forgiveness exist for the evil I do without knowing and the good I do not do? All so many questions we have to ask ourselves.

As far as transgressions against God are concerned, it depends only on me whether I am forgiven on Kippur. As far as transgressions against another person are concerned, let us quote here a few lines from Emmanuel Levinas, which cannot better conclude what has just been said, nor better open the pages that follow on God as "other":

> Let us evaluate the tremendous portent of what we have just learned. My faults toward God are forgiven without my depending on his good will! God is, in a sense, the *other, par excellence,* the other as other,

---

9. [Saint Cheron gives an extremely loose, oral translation (or commentary) of Rashi on Deuteronomy 21:8, by the chief rabbi of France, Rabbi Gilles Bernheim, which I reproduce here. Rashi actually writes: "Scripture announces to them that when they have done this (the ceremony prescribed) their sin will be forgiven."—Trans.]

the absolutely other—and nonetheless my standing with this God depends only on myself. The instrument of forgiveness is in my hands. On the other hand, my neighbor, my brother, man, infinitely less other than the absolutely other, is in a certain way more other than God. (*NT* 16)

GOD AS "OTHER" IN RELATION TO ISRAEL

After having surveyed the Jewish dimension of forgiveness in the interhuman relationship and in the Creator-creatures relationship, one other dimension needs to be examined, that in which we ask God to justify God's actions. This is a specifically Jewish dimension of the dialogue between human beings and the Holy One, blessed be He. Is it conceivable that the Almighty could have committed injustices against the world, against humanity in general, against Israel in particular, and that he himself should seek to be forgiven? It is a question that may initially appear blasphemous, yet Judaism's indisputable masters have asked themselves this very question. Several passages in the Torah were read from this perspective from the Talmud onwards. How could he who is thought of by the children of Israel as their unique Savior, the Merciful One, be guilty of any injustice whatsoever! The most famous instance of this accusation in the Torah is to be found in the book of Numbers (28:15). It concerns the burnt offerings that the children of Israel must bring regularly to HaShem, particularly on the New Moons. After the burnt offerings, the meal-offerings, and the obligatory libations, it is written, "And one male of the goats for a sin-offering to HaShem. In addition to the continual burnt-offering shall it be made, and its libation."

Read as such, this verse illustrates perfectly the fundamental necessity of having recourse to what in the

Jewish tradition we call the "obligatory" commentary by Rashi and the Talmud. And indeed readers who ignore this commentary will continue on their way, missing in truth a verse that is unique in the Torah. Here is the talmudic reading that Rashi himself relates: "The Holy One, blessed be He, said, 'Bring an atonement offering for My sake on the New Moon, because I diminished the size of the Moon.'"[10]

What is going on here? Rabbi Simeon b. Pazzi, a sage noted for his teaching, has detected a contradiction in a verse from Genesis (1:16): "'And God made the two great lights,' and immediately the verse continues 'the greater light...and the lesser light.'" He explains therefore that when God created the sun and the moon, the latter said to him, "'Sovereign of the universe! Is it possible for two kings to wear one crown?' God replied: 'Go then and make thyself smaller!'" But when he noticed that the moon was unhappy, the Holy One, blessed be He, commanded (the children of Israel only), "Bring an atonement for Me" (Tractate Hullin 60b). And Emmanuel Levinas offered the following commentary on the verse in a striking text on "Judaism and Kenosis":

> "And additionally one he-goat for a sin-offering in honor of the Eternal...." This text appears to present no difficulties—but the problem arises out of the ambiguity of the Hebrew, in which "a sin-offering in honor of the Eternal" can also be read to mean "a sin-offering on behalf of the Eternal," as if the Eternal One (God forbid!) had committed a sin to be atoned for by the sacrifice of a goat. A goat-offering for God's atonement! (*ITN* 116)

---

10. [See Rashi on Genesis 1:16, and talmudic Tractate Hullin 60b, to which Saint Cheron now turns.—Trans.]

This chain of thought may well surprise the noninitiated, but is there not here, beyond the undeniable logic, a fundamental teaching? There is no meandering in the thoughts of the *Hakhamim,* the talmudic doctors who nourished the Jewish people of the diaspora for 1,500 years and without whom there would be no Judaism today. After the sin of the Golden Calf, Elohim intended to destroy the people of Israel; it was only when Moses interceded that his pity was aroused and his anger assuaged. It is here that we find the following expression repeated several times in the Bible: "HaShem reconsidered regarding the evil that He declared He would do to His people" (Exod. 32:14).

Before broaching the problematic of the Shoah, it is important to quote George Steiner's words in a study entitled "The Long Life of Metaphor: An Approach to the 'Shoah'": "In the Shoah, the Jewish people ('Radix, Matrix')...can be seen, understood, to have died *for* God, to have taken upon itself the inconceivable guilt of God's indifference, or absence, or impotence."[11] Steiner understood long ago that if one could dare, with fear and trembling, put forward such an hypothesis, then it was in no way a question of some sin-offering for the sins of humankind. On the contrary, it was humankind's madness alone, pure hatred, literally *unpardonable,* that would have brought it about. This kind of suffering is not even the suffering of martyrs anymore: it is of an *other* order in relation to the innumerable martyrs of faith counted by history because such martyrs could deny their faith to

---

11. Steiner, "The Long Life of Metaphor," 169. [Steiner is commenting at this point on a number of poems by Paul Celan, including "Radix, Matrix."—Trans.]

save their lives, which an atheistic Jew or convert could not do.

For its part, Hasidism, the mystical movement founded at the end of the eighteenth century by the Baal Shem Tov in Central Europe, went extremely far in the idea that our forgiveness of God has to correspond to the forgiveness God grants us. "Thence the plural of *Yom Kippurim*," writes Elie Wiesel in *Souls on Fire*.[12] He also relates the following words from one of the most illustrious hasidic masters, Rabbi Levi-Yitzhak of Berditchev:

> Today is Judgment Day. David proclaims it in his Psalms. Today all Your creatures stand before You so that You may pass sentence. But I, Levi-Yitzhak, son of Sarah of Berditchev, I say and I proclaim that it is You who shall be judged today! By Your children who suffer for You, who die for You and the sanctification of Your name and Your law and Your promise.[13]

God reconsidered the evil.... It is not just the person who has committed a sin whom God redeems and forgives, he too has committed an injustice against his creation, and for which we must bring a sin-offering. In *Twilight*, Elie Wiesel has one of his characters, the mystical madman who thinks he is God, say: "I am God because I am guilty, guiltier than all human beings put together."[14] It is as if one can hear an echo and a reply—or rather a question—to Staretz Zosima's famous words in *The Brothers Karamazov*, frequently quoted by Emmanuel Levinas: "We are all guilty for everything and everyone

---

12. Wiesel, *Souls on Fire*, 107.
13. Ibid., 110.
14. Wiesel, *Twilight*, 151.

before everyone, and I more than all the others."¹⁵ So who is guiltier than everyone else, we humans or God? Faced with this universal guilt, forgiveness itself seems impotent, for what forgiveness is needed for a guilt that exceeds all reparation, all *tchouvah*?

---

15. [I follow Saint Cheron's text, which loosely cites the French Pléiade edition of Dostoyevsky's novel (310); the revised Constance Garnett translation, however, renders the Russian here as "every one of us has sinned against all men, and I more than any," with Zosima going on to say: "everyone is really responsible to all men for all men and for everything," which is more in keeping with what Levinas actually frequently quotes. See Dostoyevsky, *The Brothers Karamazov*, 268.—Trans.]

3

The Shoah
and the Unforgivable

Can one forgive the unforgivable? How can I go on trying to reflect on forgiveness without broaching the terrible question of the Shoah and beyond that of all crimes against humanity? This question is overwhelming. How can we even ask it? But how can we not ask it? The real question, after all, concerns more a deep and collective act of repentance rather than an impossible act of Jewish forgiveness. To forgive is to break one's condition of victim, it is to accept to be dispossessed of one's incurable wound, or at least what is incurable in every moral wound. But to ask for forgiveness is also difficult most of the time, inasmuch as the person who has to forget his self-esteem in his willingness to make amends, to *expiate* the wrongdoing, has to pay a price. Except that the person who is forgiving has to take upon himself to transform the wrong he has suffered into the wrong he has overcome. Every Jew, let me repeat—and no doubt every human being—must forgive the person who sincerely asks for it—and cannot in any case refuse more than three times, as we have seen previously. Unless a master is concerned.

Have we not skipped a little too quickly over one dimension of the efficiency of the forgiveness for sins committed by one man against another? The text of the Mishnah explicitly says, "for transgressions that are between a man and his fellow the Day of Atonement effects atonement only if he has appeased his fellow."[1] The important word here is "atonement," for it signifies that no forgiveness is possible without atonement. To ask for forgiveness is already to repent and as such to desire to distance oneself from the wrong one has committed. This is the first step. The second step is to obtain forgiveness, and the third is the atonement. But does this text meant only for Jews concern only Jews? Are the principles it puts forward not universal, if not universally recognized?

Here we come to an astonishing narrative by Simon Wiesenthal in his book *The Sunflower*. While a *Häftling*, a prisoner in the camp of Janowska in Lvov in Galicia, he finds himself sent one day to the Technical High School transformed into a military hospital for Nazi soldiers wounded at the front. A dying SS soldier has asked a nurse to bring him a Jew. Fate chose Simon Wiesenthal and here he is in the office he had once known as belonging to the former dean of the school in which he himself had studied architecture and now transformed into a room for a dying man. On his deathbed, the young Nazi wants to atone for his crime before he dies both by his suffering and by relating his story to the unknown Jewish deportee he has had brought in. During this surrealistic encounter

---

1. Mishnah, Tractate Yoma 8:9.

The Shoah and the Unforgivable 151

between the dying SS man and the Jew condemned to death by the Nuremburg laws, a terrifying monologue ensues. Neither can see the face of the other, since the Nazi's head is entirely wrapped in bandages. Was there ever a single such encounter like this during the whole of the war?

The young man tells Simon Wiesenthal, no doubt just as young as he is, his story from start to finish, while the latter becomes increasingly ill at ease listening to the horrifying account of the crime committed by the SS man. Brought up as a Catholic, he remained one until he joined the Hitler Youth. His mother, whom Simon Wiesenthal will meet after the war but to whom he will say nothing of her son's abominable crime, will say to him, "But one thing is certain, Karl never did any wrong.... He was such a good boy."[2]

The scene takes place in the small village of Dnyepropetrovsk in Russia.

> There were a hundred and fifty of them or perhaps two hundred, including many children who stared at us with anxious eyes. A few were quietly crying. There were infants in their mothers' arms, but hardly any young men; mostly women and greybeards.
>
> As we approached I could see the expression in their eyes—fear, indescribable fear...apparently they knew what was awaiting them....
>
> A truck arrived with cans of petrol which we unloaded and took into a house. The stronger men among the Jews were ordered to carry the cans to the upper storeys....
>
> Then we began to drive the Jews into the house.[3]

---

2. Wiesenthal, *The Sunflower,* 95, 96.
3. Ibid., 44–45.

At this point in the narrative, Simon Wiesenthal is about to leave the room. But Karl begs him to stay.

> When we were told that everything was ready, we went back a few yards, and then received the command to remove safety pins from hand grenades and throw them through the windows of the house. Detonations followed one after another...My God!...
> We heard screams and saw the flames eat their way from floor to floor....We had our rifles ready to shoot down anyone who tried to escape from the blazing hell....
> The screams from the house were horrible.[4]

Reliving the horror, the dying young SS man's whole body convulses, and Wiesenthal adds: "I saw that he was summoning his strength for one last effort to tell me the rest of the story to its bitter end." Karl's narrative proceeds after he has pleaded with his "guest" one more time to wait until the end.

> "Behind the windows of the second floor, I saw a man with a small child in his arms. His clothes were alight. By his side stood a woman, doubtless the mother of the child. With his free hand the man covered the child's eyes—then he jumped into the street. Seconds later the mother followed. Then from the other windows fell burning bodies...We shot...Oh God!"

The dying man held his hand in front of his bandaged eyes as if he wanted to banish the picture from his mind.

"I don't know how many tried to jump out of the windows but that one family I shall never

---

4. Ibid., 46.

forget—least of all the child. It had black hair and dark eyes."⁵

A few days later, during an attack on the enemy, a shell explodes next to Karl. After his operation,

> The pain became more and more unbearable. My whole body is covered with marks from pain-killing injections.... That was the real punishment for me....
> The pains in my body are terrible, but worse still is my conscience. It never ceases to remind me of the burning house and the family that jumped from the window.⁶

And he adds these words with which he desperately seeks to atone for his unspeakable crime:

> Believe me, I would be ready to suffer worse and longer pains if by that means I could bring back the dead, at Dnyepropetrovsk.... But I... I am left here with my guilt. In the last hours of my life you are with me. I do not know who you are, I only know that you are a Jew and that is enough.⁷

To this confession torn from his last dying breath, the German adds nothing but a prayer addressed to Simon Wiesenthal:

> I know what I have told you is terrible. In the long nights while I have been waiting for death, time and time again I have longed to talk about it to a Jew and beg forgiveness from him. Only I didn't know whether there were any Jews left.

---

5. Ibid., 46–47.
6. Ibid., 55, 56.
7. Ibid., 57.

> "I know that what I am asking is almost too much for you, but without your answer I cannot die in peace."...
> Two men who had never known each other had been brought together for a few hours by Fate. One asks the other for help. But the other was himself helpless and able to do nothing for him. I stood up and looked in his direction, at his folded hands. Between them there seemed to rest a sunflower.
> At last I made up my mind and without a word I left the room.[8]

Simon Wiesenthal's entire narrative poses in an extremely meaningful way the question of evil, which it would be tempting to call metaphysical evil were it not paradoxically to attribute a metaphysical power to the theoreticians of the Final Solution. The unseen face of the child with black hair and dark eyes symbolizes the eternally absolute enigma posed by the destruction of a million and a half Jewish children. What Simon Wiesenthal did was all that a sensible and responsible being could do in all conscience, in other words in thinking of the victims and not just of himself. He did everything it was in his power to do. The rest was not his to do. The rest was for the dead. He will have been the Jewish hand, no doubt the last hand that Karl S. will have held. He was the only one to have heard the dying SS man's confession. And when asked for forgiveness, he did only what he could do. He replied with silence, better than saying no.

---

8. Ibid., 57, 58.

Forgiving and Forgetting

In the second part of the book, Simon Wiesenthal insisted on publishing the reactions of numerous known or lesser known personalities, from Primo Levi to Léopold Sédar Senghor, from René Cassin to Gustav W. Heinemann, the former president of the Bundesrepublik and one of the few to have considered the encounter with the mother to be in a certain way as important as that with her son. Simon Wiesenthal ends the account of this visit with the following sentence: "I took my leave without diminishing in any way the poor woman's last surviving consolation—faith in the goodness of her son."[9] Not to shatter the last hopes, the last memories of Karl's mother, this he felt, *despite himself,* he had the right to do.

At the end of his reply, Gustav W. Heinemann writes, "The conflict between Justice (in the form of Law) and Forgiveness is the thread that runs through your story. Justice and Law, however essential they are, cannot exist without Forgiveness. That is the quality that Jesus Christ added to Justice and with which He gave it life."[10] By what prerogative did the Nazarene annul what Moses established? If God himself cannot forgive the wrong of one man committed against his fellow—and is the word "wrong" here not tragically inadequate?—by what authority would Jesus do so? But Jesus in fact did not forgive; he said, rather that "blasphemy against the Holy Ghost shall not be forgiven unto men" (Matt. 12:31). Was the Shoah—and perhaps all forms of genocide—not "blasphemy against the Holy Ghost"?

---

9. Ibid., 95.
10. Ibid., 129–30.

Jews and Christians can be reconciled in any case through the words of Jacques Maritain: "I could forgive you only for any wrong you might have done to me personally. How, though, could I, in their name, forgive you for the atrocities you committed against others? What you have done is, humanly speaking, unforgivable. But *in the name of your God,* yes, I forgive you."[11] The reply by Martin Niemoeller, who was president of the Evangelical Church of Hesse-Nassau and founder of an association "that gave birth to the resistance movement of the Protestant Churches against Nazism," is even closer to Judaism when he writes to Simon Wiesenthal:

> The Christian that I am—or at least try to be—when faced with one of his fellows who would lay bare his tortured conscience before him, could only reply the following, but he would be obligated to do so: "The wrong you have done me and for which you repent now, I forgive you as I myself am freed by the forgiveness I receive. The wrong you have done others, others who are close to me and whose suffering affects me too, they are the ones who will have to forgive you, or someone else who has full powers to do so, which is not my case."[12]

What is most serious in the reproach leveled at Simon Wiesenthal by Gustav W. Heinemann is to place him on the side of justice and law, opposed no less to forgiveness. Nothing could be further from the truth, for does it not already presuppose that the dead have no need either of law or justice, and that one needs to go beyond

---

11. Ibid., 171.
12. [Martin Niemoeller's reply is not included in the English translation of *The Sunflower.*—Trans.]

The Shoah and the Unforgivable 157

them in order to absolve the executioners? Was it not because of this that not one Nazi criminal judged by a (West) German court was condemned to death before the abolition of the death sentence in 1949? A curious form of mercy that forgives without angst in place of the victims. We may well ask, moreover, if this conception of forgiveness is even Christian. Where is it written that you will forgive in place of the victims and martyrs? Would not the repentant executioner, therefore, come before the victim? Which amounts to saying that the Nazi who makes atonement is more praiseworthy than the Jew or Gypsy he tortured. A religion for guilty repentants more than for victims. In his talmudic reading "As Old as the World?," Emmanuel Levinas wrote, "I think...that the sages of the Talmud opposed practices which encroached upon the rights of hell: for whatever the rights of charity may be, a place had to be foreseen and kept warm for all eternity for Hitler and his followers. Without a hell for evil, nothing in the world would make sense any longer" (*NT* 87).

According to Christian moral theology, a criminal who is not aware of his sin can subjectively have been innocent. This is not the case in Judaism, since at one point in our page from the Tractate Yoma, the question is raised concerning the transgressions for which we are guilty without having been aware we committed them—and for which atonement has to be made. Two more commentaries on the replies to Simon Wiesenthal. Luise Rinser, a Christian who was imprisoned by the Gestapo, asks him the following intolerable question: "Were you authorised by your people *not* to forgive? No. Perhaps you acted against the wish of the dead Jews. I hope that those dead Jews will grant you 'extenuating circumstances' in view of the difficulty of the case."[13] Is this not an unjust judgment? On the evening of his encounter, Wiesenthal told his closest friends in the hut about his attitude toward the dying SS man. One of them, Josek, "a deeply religious Jew," said to him,

> Do you know,...when you were telling us about your meeting with the SS man, I feared at first, that you had really forgiven him. You would have had no right to do this in the name of the people who had not authorised you to do so. What people have done to you yourself, you can, if you like, forgive and forget. That is your own affair. But it would have been a terrible sin to burden your conscience with other people's sufferings.[14]

Luise Rinse and Josek, killed with a bullet because he "was too weak even to stand up,"[15] did not consider the reality of evil and forgiveness from the same point of view. For Josek would certainly have "shuddered" if he could have read this sentence from the German psychologist: "I shudder at the thought that you let that *repentant* young man go to his death without a word of forgiveness."[16] The fact remains that Josek died, murdered, and that he would not have wanted anyone to feel authorized to forgive in his name.

Who can burden one's conscience with other people's suffering, with the suffering of victims and martyrs? This is the gaping question from the bottomless depths of the Shoah. Who, if not the Messiah? Unless it were Eliyahu HaNavi, the prophet Elijah, the precursor to the Messiah

---

13. In Wiesenthal, *The Sunflower,* 198.
14. Ibid., 68.
15. Ibid., 79.
16. Ibid., 198.

dear to our tradition? But why not the Holy One, blessed be He, himself? Elie Wiesel once told me when I asked him about the ability of the Messiah to bear the suffering of the Shoah whose "monstrous enormity," going beyond the limits of human understanding, has turned it into the paradigm of all political suffering: "The coming of the Messiah will not necessarily bring a reply to this immense and unjustifiable suffering.... We have not made a theology of suffering... and to make suffering into a theology is almost to justify it, and we have no right to do that."[17]

Here, we need to open a parenthesis. Speaking one day about the Jews who had died during the Shoah, Cardinal Jean-Marie Lustiger went so far as to think out loud things that at all events, as Emmanuel Levinas says, cannot be preached: "I think that somewhere those who died belong to the Messiah's suffering. But God alone can say so, not me. And that one day, those who persecuted them will recognize that it is thanks to them that we are saved." In one go, we see the Passion of the Jews assimilated and mixed with Jesus' suffering, despite themselves. A redemptive Passion that fails to take into account the "despair—and perhaps the doubts—of those who were going to die."[18] After which, their agony, their mortal nameless anguish, their martyrdom, would be the very condition of salvation—for the executioners. What a marvelous turnaround where forgiveness—or more exactly, salvation—the redemption of the executioners, is the work of the victims *despite themselves*. Even in their ignominious death, would they still be victims, posthumous converts, redeeming a wrong they neither sought

---

17. In Saint Cheron, *Le mal et l'exil*, 260, 262.
18. Levinas, "L'essentiel vient d'être dit...," 16.

nor desired, but which carried them off in a state of infinite dereliction, without the shadow of a theological justification, with no meaning, no possible hope, and, finally, no forgiveness? Just as in Judaism there is no forgiveness by proxy, so there can be no redemption by proxy. It is very rare for those who are murdered to have the necessary distance to forgive their killers who do not ask for it. But are not the martyrs of Auschwitz and of the Shoah *other* in relation to the victims of human barbarity? Yet can we even think this after the genocides in Cambodia and Rwanda?

What the survivors of the Shoah teach us is that this crime is literally *unpardonable*. It exceeds all soul-searching and individual forms of forgiveness. The president of the German Republic or the chancellor can certainly ask for forgiveness from the State of Israel as the symbol of the Jewish people, united and politically and historically undivided. And the State of Israel can accept the request, but in the name of the living, not of the dead. The forgiveness granted by a state to another state would in a sense be to remove the guilt from the children of the executioners, putting into practice the Torah's teaching that children are not responsible for the crimes of their parents. But just as I can forgive only for what I have personally suffered, so can I forgive only the person who has acted against me. Here too, there can be no intermediary. Forgiveness in either case cannot be given by proxy. Which means that in the most favorable case where the victim and the executioner are still alive, the former can forgive only if the latter asks for it.

There are always two people needed for forgiveness; if one is missing, there is no possibility for forgiveness. No one can forgive against the guilty party's conscience. As it happens, would not the imprescriptibility of the

The Shoah and the Unforgivable 161

Nazi crimes have a theological meaning? We can hear Vladimir Jankélévitch's cry incessantly rising from the depths of oblivion: "Lord, do not forgive them, for they know what they do."[19] Let us quote again from his book *L'imprescriptible* [*The Imprescriptible*], when he warns against those who would tend to confuse forgiving and forgetting: "Today, when the sophists recommend that we forget,...we will think hard of the agony of the deportees who knew no burial and of the children who never came back. For this agony will last for all eternity."[20]

This is why the whole question of erecting buildings for Catholic worship on these sites stems from both the fear that the Jewish specificity of the Shoah should be lost and the fear that an atonement by proxy—for monsters who asked for nothing, with a few exceptions—would lead to a gratuitous, and thus absurd forgiving and forgetting. "Free forgiveness is always at the expense of someone innocent who does not receive it" (*BV* 104), writes Emmanuel Levinas.

If Judaism is essential to the world—for all it has given to humankind over thousands of years of holy history—it is surely also because it alone—or almost—thought that forgiveness was rarely played out just between two people but rather between three, with an excluded third, and that this excluded third—simply absent or perhaps dead...murdered—could not be forgotten. Which is why forgiveness is inseparable from justice, so no one is left out, failing which there would be no true forgiveness but simply "consolations that cost us nothing and compassion without suffering" (*PN* 16).

---

19. Jankélévitch, *L'imprescriptible*, 43.
20. Ibid., 62–63.

Bibliography

EMMANUEL LEVINAS

"A Language Familiar to Us." Trans. Douglas Collins. *Telos* 44 (1980): 199–201.—"Un langage pour nous familier." *Le Matin,* special issue (1980); reprinted in *Les Imprévus de l'histoire.* Montpellier: Fata Morgana, 1994, 149–54.

Alterity and Transcendence. Trans. Michael B. Smith. London: The Athlone Press, 1999.—*Altérité et transcendance.* Montpellier: Fata Morgana, 1995.

"Amour et révélation." In *La charité aujourd'hui.* Conference of theologians, organized by the Association for the Jean-Rodhain Foundation. Paris: Éditions SOS, 1981, 133–48.

Basic Philosophical Writings. Ed. Adriaan T. Peperzak, Simon Critchley, and Robert Bernasconi. Bloomington: Indiana University Press, 1996.

"Being Jewish." Trans. Mary Beth Mader. *Continental Philosophy Review* 40 (2007): 205–10.—"Être Juif." *Confluences* 15–17 (1947); reprinted in *Les cahiers d'études lévinassiennes* 1 (2002): 99–106.

Beyond the Verse: Talmudic Readings and Lectures. Trans. Gary D. Mole. London: The Athlone Press, 1994; reprinted edition: New York: Continuum, 2007.—*L'au-delà du verset: Lectures et discours talmudiques.* Paris: Minuit, 1982.

Difficult Freedom: Essays on Judaism. Trans. Seán Hand. Baltimore: The Johns Hopkins University Press, 1990.—*Difficile liberté: Essais sur le judaïsme.* Paris: Albin Michel, 1963, new revised edition, 1976.

Discovering Existence with Husserl. Trans. Richard A. Cohen and Michael B. Smith. Evanston, Ill.: Northwestern University Press, 1998.—*En découvrant l'existence avec Husserl et Heidegger.* Paris: Vrin, 1949.

Entre Nous: On Thinking-of-the-Other. Trans. Michael B. Smith and Barbara Harshav. London: The Athlone Press, 1998.—*Entre nous: Essais sur le penser-à-l'autre*. Paris: Grasset, 1991.

"L'essentiel vient d'être dit..." *Les Nouveaux Cahiers* 85 (Summer 1986): 15–17.

Ethics and Infinity: Conversations with Philippe Nemo. Trans. Richard A. Cohen. Pittsburgh: Duquesne University Press, 1985.—*Ethique et infini*. Paris: Librairie Arthème Fayard et Radio France, 1982.

Existence and Existents. Trans. Alphonso Lingis. The Hague: Martinus Nijhoff, 1978.—*De l'existence à l'existant*. Paris: Fontaine, 1947.

"Existentialism and Anti-Semitism." Trans. Denis Hollier and Rosalind Krauss. *October* 87 (Winter 1999): 27–31.—"Existentialisme et antisémitisme." *Les Cahiers de l'Alliance Israélite Universelle* 14–15 (1947); reprinted in *Les imprévus de l'histoire*. Montpellier: Fata Morgana, 1994, 119–22.

God, Death, and Time. Trans. Bettina Bergo. Stanford: Stanford University Press, 2000.—*Dieu, la mort et le temps*. Paris: Grasset, 1993.

Humanism of the Other. Trans. Nidra Poller. Urbana: University of Illinois Press, 2003.—*Humanisme de l'autre homme*. Montpellier: Fata Morgana, 1972.

In the Time of the Nations. Trans. Michael B. Smith. London: The Athlone Press, 1994.—*À l'heure des nations*. Paris: Minuit, 1988.

Is It Righteous to Be? Interviews with Emmanuel Levinas. Ed. Jill Robbins. Stanford: Stanford University Press, 2001.

"Mitgenommen." In *Honneur aux maîtres*. Ed. Marguerite Léna. Paris: Critérion, 1991, 227–28.

New Talmudic Readings. Trans. Richard A. Cohen. Pittsburgh: Duquesne University Press, 1999.—*Nouvelles lectures talmudiques*. Paris: Minuit, 1996.

Nine Talmudic Readings. Trans. Annette Aronowicz. Bloomington: Indiana University Press, 1990.—*Quatre lectures talmudiques*. Paris: Minuit, 1968; and *Du sacré au saint. Cinq nouvelles lectures talmudiques*. Paris: Minuit, 1977.

Of God Who Comes to Mind. Trans. Bettina Bergo. Stanford: Stanford University Press, 1998.—*De Dieu qui vient à l'idée.* Paris: Vrin, 1982.

On Escape: De l'évasion. Trans. Bettina Bergo. Stanford: Stanford University Press, 2003.—"De l'évasion." *Recherches Philosophiques* (1935); reprinted in *De l'évasion.* Montpellier: Fata Morgana, 1982.

Otherwise Than Being or Beyond Essence. Trans. Alphonso Lingis. Pittsburgh: Duquesne University Press, 2006.—*Autrement qu'être ou au-dela de l'essence.* The Hague: Martinus Nijhoff, 1974.

Outside the Subject. Trans. Michael B. Smith. Stanford: Stanford University Press, 1994.—*Hors sujet.* Montpellier: Fata Morgana, 1987.

Proper Names. Trans. Michael B. Smith. Stanford: Stanford University Press, 1996. *Noms propres.*—Montpellier: Fata Morgana, 1976.

"Reflections on the Philosophy of Hitlerism." Trans. Seán Hand. *Critical Inquiry* 17, no. 1 (Autumn 1990): 63–71.—"Quelques réflexions sur la philosophie de l'hitlérisme." *Esprit* 26 (1934); reprinted in *Les imprévus de l'histoire.* Montpellier: Fata Morgana, 1994, 27–41.

The Theory of Intuition in Husserl's Phenomenology. Trans. André Orianne. Evanston: Northwestern University Press, 1973.— *Théorie de l'intuition dans la phénoménologie de Husserl.* Paris: Alcan, 1930.

Time and the Other. Trans. Richard A. Cohen. Pittsburgh: Duquesne University Press, 1987.—"Le temps et l'autre." *Cahiers du Collège Philosophique* 1 (1948); reprinted in *Le temps et l'autre.* Montpellier: Fata Morgana, 1979.

Totality and Infinity: An Essay on Exteriority. Trans. Alphonso Lingis. Pittsburgh: Duquesne University Press, 2007.—*Totalité et infini: Essai sur l'extériorité.* The Hague: Martinus Nijhoff, 1961.

Jewish Religious Texts

ArtScroll Machzor Rosh Hashanah. Nusach Sefard. A New Translation and Anthologized Commentary by Rabbi Nosson Scherman. New York: Mesorah Publications, 1994.

Bibliography 165

ArtScroll Machzor Yom Kippur. Nusach Sefard. A New Translation and Anthologized Commentary by Rabbi Nosson Scherman. New York: Mesorah Publications, 1994.

ArtScroll Tanach. The Stone Edition. Ed. Rabbi Nosson Scherman. New York: Mesorah Publications, 2000.

The Babylonian Talmud. Ed. Isidore Epstein. 34 vols. London: The Soncino Press, 1935–1952.

Chumash. With Rashi's Commentary. 5 vols. Ed. and trans. Rabbi A. M. Silbermann. New York and Jerusalem: Feldheim Publishers, 1985.

Hayyim de Volozhyn. *L'âme de la vie: Nefesh HaHayyim*. Trans. Benjamin Gross. Lagrasse: Verdier, 1986.

Kitov, Eliyahu. *The Book of Our Heritage*. 3 vols. Trans. Nathan Bulman. New York and Jerusalem: Feldheim Publishers, 1988.

Midrash Tanchuma. The Metsudah Midrash Tanchuma. Hebrew-English. Trans. Rabbi Avrohom Davis. New York: Eastern Book Press, 2004–2005.

The Mishnah. Trans. Herbert Danby. Oxford: Oxford University Press, 1992.

Secondary Works

Arendt, Hannah. *Journal de pensée (1950–1973)*. 2 vols. Paris: Seuil, 2005.

Blanchot, Maurice. "Ce qu'il nous a appris." *L'Arche* 459 (February 1996), 68.

Boblet-Viart, Marie-Hélène, ed. "Roman 20–50." Spécial André Malraux. *Revue d'étude du roman du XXe siècle* (June 1995).

Buber, Martin. *Meetings: Autobiographical Fragments*. New York: Routledge, 2002.

Calin, Rodolphe, and François-David Sebbah, *Le vocabulaire de Levinas*. Paris: Ellipses, 2002.

Cazenave, Michel, ed. *André Malraux: Cahier de l'Herne*. Paris: L'Herne, 1982.

Celan, Paul. *Breathturn*. Trans. Pierre Joris. Los Angeles: Green Integer, 2006.

Confucius. *The Analects*. Trans. Raymond Dawson. Oxford: Oxford University Press, 2000.

——. *Entretiens avec Confucius*. Trans. Anne Cheng. Paris: Seuil, 1981.

Derrida, Jacques. *Adieu to Emmanuel Levinas*. Trans. Pascale-Anne Brault and Michael Naas. Stanford: Stanford University Press, 1999.

——. "Entretien inédit avec Roger-Pol Droit." *Le Monde*, October 12, 2004, III.

——. *Writing and Difference*. Trans. Alan Bass. London: Routledge, 1997.

Dostoyevsky, Fyodor. *The Brothers Karamazov*. Trans. Constance Garnett, revised Ralph E. Matlaw. New York: W. W. Norton, 1976.

Dumas, Jean-Louis. *Histoire de la pensée: Philosophies et philosophes*. vol. 3, *Temps modernes*. Paris: Le Livre de poche, 1993.

Foucault, Michel. *Le courage de la vérité. Le Gouvernement de soi et des autres*, vol. 2. Paris: Gallimard/Seuil, 2009.

Heidegger, Martin. *What Is That—Philosophy?* Trans. Eva T. H. Brann. Annapolis, Md.: St. John's College, 1991.

——. *Zollikon Seminars: Protocols—Conversations—Letters*. Trans. Franz Mayr and Richard Askay. Evanston, Ill.: Northwestern University Press, 2001.

Jankélévitch, Vladimir. *L'imprescriptible*. Paris: Seuil, 1986.

Kafka, Franz. *Oeuvres complètes*. Vol. 3. Trans. Marthe Robert, Claude David, and Jean-Pierre Danès. Paris: Gallimard, Collection Bibliothèque de la Pléiade, 1984.

——. *The Penguin Complete Short Stories of Franz Kafka*. Ed. Nahum N. Glazer. Trans. Willa and Edwin Muir. Harmondsworth: Penguin Book, 1983.

Levy, Karen. *André Malraux: D'un siècle l'autre*. Paris: Gallimard, 2002.

Malraux, André. *L'homme précaire et la littérature*. Paris: Gallimard, 1977.

——. *Lazarus*. Trans. Terence Kilmartin. New York: Holt, Rinehart and Winston, 1977.

——. *La légende du siècle*. Documentary directed by Claude Santelli, 1972.

——. *Man's Fate*. Trans. Haakon M. Chevalier. New York: Vintage Books, 1961.

——. *Les métamorphoses du regard*. Four previously unreleased films by Clovis Prévost [1973]. With DVD. Paris: Maeght, 2006.

——. "Radioscopie de Jacques Chancel." *France Inter*, March 7, 1974.

——. *The Royal Way*. Trans. Stuart Gilbert. New York: Random House, n.d.

——. "Texte liminaire." In *Israël. Introductory text*. Lausanne: La Guilde du Livre et Éditions Clairefontaine, 1955, 7–11.

——. *The Walnut Trees of Altenburg*. Trans. A. W. Fielding. Chicago: The University of Chicago Press, 1992.

Mencius, *Mencius*. Trans. David Hinton. Washington: Counterpoint, 1999.

Picon, Gaëtan. *Malraux par lui-même*. Paris: Seuil, 1953.

Plato. *Gorgias*. Trans. Robin Waterfield. Oxford: Oxford University Press, 2008.

Ricoeur, Paul. *Autrement*. Paris: PUF, 1997.

——. *Oneself as Another*. Trans. Kathleen Blamey. Chicago: The University of Chicago Press, 1992.

Rolland, Jacques. *Parcours de l'autrement: Lecture d'Emmanuel Levinas*. Paris: PUF, 2000.

Rosenzweig, Franz. *The Star of Redemption*. Trans. Barbara Ellen Galli. Madison: The University of Wisconsin Press, 2004.

Saint Cheron, Michaël de. "Entretien avec Paul Ricoeur." *Bulletin du Centre Protestant d'Études* 43, no. 7 (November 1991): 7–27.

——. *Le mal et l'exil, dix ans après: Entretiens avec Elie Wiesel*. Paris: Nouvelle Cité, 1999.

——. *De la mémoire à la responsabilité*. Paris: Éditions Dervy, 2000.

Saint Cheron, Philippe, Xavier de Chalendar, and Nassib Mahfouz. *Le pardon*. Paris: Éditions du Centurion, 1992.

Sartre, Jean-Paul. "*Aminadab*, or the Fantastic Considered as a Language." In *Literary and Philosophical Essays*. Trans. Annette Michelson. London: Hutchinson, 1968, 56–72.

———. *Being and Nothingness*. Trans. Hazel E. Barnes. London: Routledge, 2000.

Sartre, Jean-Paul, and Benny Lévy. *Hope Now: The 1980 Interviews*. Trans. Adrian van den Hoven. Chicago: The University of Chicago Press, 1996.

Spinoza, Baruch. *Ethics*. Ed. and trans. G. H. R. Parkinson. Oxford: Oxford University Press, 2000.

Steiner, George. "The Long Life of Metaphor: An Approach to the 'Shoah.'" In *Writing and the Holocaust*. Ed. Berel Lang. New York: Holmes and Meier, 1988, 154–71.

Tornay, Alain. *L'oubli du bien: La réponse de Levinas*. Preface by André de Muralt. Genève: Slatkine, 1999.

Vázquez Moro, Ulpiano. *El Discurso sobre Dios en la obra de Emmanuel Levinas*. Madrid: Publicaciones de la Universidad Pontificia Comillas, 1982.

Villani, Sergio. "Malraux-Israël: Retour à la Genèse." Unpublished conference paper delivered at the Conference for the Twentieth Anniversary of the Death of Malraux, Paris, Sorbonne, 1996.

Wiesel, Elie. *Souls on Fire: Portraits and Legends of Hasidic Masters*. Trans. Marion Wiesel. New York: Vintage Books, 1972.

———. *Twilight*. Trans. Marion Wiesel. New York: Summit, 1988.

Wiesenthal, Simon. *The Sunflower*. Trans. H. A. Piehler. New York: Schocken Books, 1976.

Zaklad, Jean. *Pour une éthique*. Lagrasse: Verdier, 1979.

Zarader, Jean-Pierre. *Malraux ou la pensée sur l'art*. Paris: Ellipses, 1998.

Index

Note: Footnotes are indicated by *n* following a page number.

Aaron, 35
Abba, Rabbi Hiyya b., 136
Abbahu, Rabbi, 139
Abel, 133–35
Abraham, 123
Adam, 77, 81, 114, 126, 135
Adorno, Theodor, 92
agnosticism, 72, 74–76, 84–85, 87
Akiba, Rabbi, 29–30, 137, 141
Alliance Israélite Universelle, 53
Alterity and Transcendence (Levinas), 79
"Amour et révélation" (Levinas), 48
anti-Semitism, 16, 31–32, 44, 52, 53
Aquinas, Thomas, 7, 75
Arendt, Hannah, 51
Aristotle, 7, 92
Ark of the Covenant, 139
Armenia, 93
art, and death, 89
atheism, 72, 74, 85, 87
atomic weapons, 19, 99
atonement, 150–54
Augustine, Saint, 7, 86
Auschwitz, xii*n*, 8, 32, 99
Azariah, Rabbi Eleazar b., 137, 138

Baal Shem Tov, 146
Bach, Johann Sebastian, *Et expecto*, 80
Balthazar, Hans Urs von, xii, 13
Beethoven, Ludwig van, *Ninth Symphony*, 80
Begin, Menachem, 55
being, 42–50; "event of being," 43, 86, 102; "otherwise than being," 43–44, 47, 86, 94, 96. *See also* ontology
Ben Patura, 29–30
Bergson, Henri, xi, 8, 27–28, 38, 46, 86, 93–95, 103; *Time and Free Will*, 93
Bernheim, Rabbi Gilles, 142*n*
biblical interpretation, 15. *See also* Jewish commentary, Levinas's
Blanchot, Maurice, 51; *Aminadab*, 57
Brahms, Johannes, *First Symphony*, 80
Buber, Martin, 14–15, 99
Buddhism, 69

Cain, 127, 133–35
Cambodia, 80, 93, 99
capital punishment. *See* death penalty
Carmelite nuns, 31–32
Cassin, René, 155
Catholic Church, 19
Celan, Paul, 62
Cheng, Anne, 50
China, 93
Chinese philosophy, 42, 50
Christianity: on death, 69; and forgiveness, 138, 155–57; and hostage, 24; Judaism and, xvi, 13–14; Levinas's attitude toward, 6, 33; and Levinas's

170   Index

thought, xii, 5, 24, 33, 49–50; and philosophy, 7
Clément, Olivier, 6
cogito, 56
Communism, 19–21
Confucius, 42, 50
culpability, 58, 79

Daniel, 32
Dante Alighieri, 38
Dao, 42
Dasein, 2
David, 136
death: and atonement, 129–30; concept of, 71–72; ethics and, 90; faith and, 69–72; as fundamental question, 48, 69–70, 75, 89; impenetrability of, 69–74, 83–84; Judaism and, 60, 68; Levinas on, 26–27, 70–72, 75; Malraux and, 71–84, 88–90; and nothingness, 26–27, 70–71, 75; objectivity of, 71–72; "otherwise than being" and, 44; religions and, 69–71; and revelation, 71–74, 83–84. *See also* dying for
"Death and Time" (Levinas), 72
death penalty, 130, 137, 141
Decourtray, Albert, 19, 19*n*
De Gaulle, Charles, 7
Derrida, Jacques, 3, 45, 97–98; "Adieu," xiv, 3, 108–09; "Violence and Metaphysics," xiv
Descartes, René, 38, 42, 46, 50, 95, 99
desire, 103
Deuteronomy, 140
Difficult Freedom (Levinas), 14
Discovering Existence with Husserl (Levinas), 46
disinterestedness, 17–18, 22
Dostoyevsky, Fyodor, 8; *The Brothers Karamazov,* 146–47
drash (symbolic meaning), 131
Dumas, Jean-Louis, 46
duration, 94, 103
dying for, 5–6, 24–25, 90. *See also* sacrifice

École normale israélite orientale (ENIO), 1
Eden, 81
Eichmann, Adolf, 137, 141
Elijah, 158
Elkaïm-Sartre, Arlette, 62
Enlightenment, 94
Entre Nous (Levinas), 9, 87
epiphany, 46–47, 78–84, 99, 104
Eros: and exteriority, 102; and the future, 29; and intersubjectivity, 101–02. *See also* love
Esther, 5, 24, 25
ethics: Chinese, 42, 50; criticism of, 17–18; and death, 90; face of the other and, 80; as first philosophy, 3, 51, 56, 79, 88, 94, 98, 108; and God, 32–33, 84–85; and hostage, 23–24; Judaism and, 60–61; Levinas's notion of, xi, 32–33, 51, 86; Ricoeur and, 4–5; sacrifice and, 9; temporality and, 8
Eve, 81, 126, 135
event of being, 43, 86, 102
evil, 134–35, 143–47, 154
Existence and Existents (Levinas), 101
Exodus, book of, 127
exteriority, 100–01

face of the other: defined, 47–48; desire and, 103; epiphany of, 47, 78–80, 99, 104; ethics and, 80; and exteriority, 100; God and, 33–34, 85, 86; justice and, 30; the nature of seeing, 33–34; philosophy and, 103; and transcendence, 82, 104–05
faith: agnosticism and, 74–75; and death, 69–72
feelings, 29, 91
feminine, the, 29, 48–50
Feuerbach, Ludwig, 97
Finkielkraut, Alain, 4
folly, opposition to, 41–42
forgiveness, xv–xvi; Christianity and, 138, 155–57; in Hebrew, 118–19; Judaism and, 116–19,

123–24, 126–31, 149–61; justice and, 155, 161; questions concerning, 142; Shoah and, 149–61; sin and, 127; for transgressions against God, 128, 135, 138–40, 142; for transgressions against humans, 128, 135–36, 138–42, 149–50, 160; universality of, 116; vengeance opposed to, 136; Yom Kippur and, 116–19, 138–40, 142 for-itself, 59
Foucault, Michel, 42, 96n6
freedom, 56–57, 94, 134
French language, "forgiveness" in, 118–19
Fumet, Stanislas, 14

Gaon of Vilna (Elijah ben Shlomo Zalman), 130
Gemara, 139
Genesis, book of, 144
genocides, 47–48, 80, 93, 99, 160. *See also* Shoah
Gibeonites, 136
God: in Cain and Abel story, 133–34; as cruel/vengeful, 126–27; ethics and, 32–33, 84–85; and evil, 134, 143–47; face of the other and, 33–34, 85, 86; and forgiveness, 128, 135, 138–40, 142, 146; holiness and, 23, 85; humans in relation to, 8, 26, 84, 134; humans' knowledge of, 72, 74–75, 82–83; Israel in relation to, 63–64, 131, 143–47; law and, 35; Levinas on, xii, 8, 16, 32, 42, 84–85; *mitzvah* and, 33; and the other, 86; as other, 142–47; sins against, 126–29, 135, 138–40, 142; as the third, 34, 35; and Torah, 25; "who comes to mind," xiv, 3, 8, 33, 46, 50, 90, 107–08. *See also* transcendence
Goethe, Johann Wolfgang von, 38
Golden Calf, 123, 145
Good, the, 45, 50, 95–96, 104, 107

guilt, 35, 146–47, 157
Gulag, 99

hagibor (mighty), 32
Hakhamim (talmudic sages), 137, 145
Hanina, Rabbi Jose b., 140
hanora (awesome), 32
Hasidism, 146
Hebrew language, "forgiveness" in, 118–19
Hegel, G. W. F., 4, 20, 61–63, 65, 99; *Phenomenology of Mind*, 93, 95
Heidegger, Martin, xi, 3, 44; and being, xiii, 45–46, 95, 98–99, 104; *Being and Time*, 93, 99; and care, 36; criticism of, 5, 50, 88, 90; and death, 27, 88, 90; Levinas and, 46, 93–94, 109; and metaphysics, 2, 104; and thinking, 91–92; and time, 27–28
Heinemann, Gustav W., 155–56
Helbe, Rabbi Joseph b., 139
Hinduism, 66, 69
Hiroshima, 99
history: end of, 20–21; Hegelian concept of, 61–63, 65; Judaism and, 61–68, 113; Levinas and, xii; totality of, 61, 63. *See also* time
Hitlerism. *See* Nazism
holiness: defining, 18, 22–24; and God, 23, 85; and hostage, 23–24; and human-God relationship, 84; human relations and, 22; and justice, 48–49; *kadosh* and, 18, 24, 49; Levinas's notion of, xiv, 3, 5, 41–42, 48–49, 51–52; philosophy and, 108; responsibility and, 17; sacredness vs., 88
Holocaust. *See* Shoah
hope, 9, 28, 70
Hosea, 125
hostage, 23–24, 36–37, 50, 106
Humanism and the Other (Levinas), 55
humanism of the other, xvi, 109

humanity: dangers to, 19, 95; folly of, 8; God in relation to, 8, 26, 84, 134; history and, 20–21; holiness of, 42; Jewish history and, 65, 67–68; and the other, 33, 36, 47, 79–80; politics and, 18; responsibility of, 27; transcendent capacity of, 9, 48, 74
human relations, 21–22. See also reciprocity
human uncondition, 66
Husserl, Edmund, 46, 63, 70, 93, 95, 109

immanence, 33
incarnation, 33, 87
infinite, the, 99, 103
Inquisition, 117
intentionality, 93
intercession, 123
intersubjectivity, 101–02
Iraq, 19
Islam, 134
Israel: collectivity of, 123, 124; death penalty in, 137, 141; and forgiveness for Shoah, 160; God in relation to, 64, 131, 143–47; and history, 61
I-Thou, 99

Jankélévitch, Vladimir, 45, 161
Jaspers, Karl, 97
Jeremiah, 32
Jesus, 155, 159
"Jewish Being" (Levinas), 65
Jewish commentary, Levinas's, 1, 8, 29–31, 121, 136, 144, 157. See also biblical interpretation
Jews. See Israel; Judaism; Shoah
Jews of Kippur, 117
Johanan, Rabbi, 136
John Paul II, Pope, 31–32
Jonah, 116
Judaism: Christianity and, 13–14; and ethics, 60–61; and forgiveness, 116–19, 123–24, 126–31, 149–61; Hegel and, 61–62; and history, 61–68, 113; Levinas and, xii, 13–14, 88, 107; and philosophy, 107; post-Christian, xii, 13–14; and responsibility, 114–16, 120; Sartre and, 60–68; special character of, 65–67, 115–16; and universality, 114–16, 120. See also Shoah
"Judaism and Kenosis" (Levinas), 144
justice: and the defendant, 30–31; forgiveness and, 155, 161; holiness and, 48–49; and the third party, 106
justification for living, xi, 7–8, 77

kadosh, 18, 24, 49
Kafka, Franz, 35, 57–59, 70, 72–73, 126; Diary, 73; Before the Law, 59
Kant, Immanuel, 3, 74, 86, 95, 103; Critique of Pure Reason, 93; Foundation of the Metaphysics of Morals, 51
kavanah (intention), 122
Kierkegaard, Søren, 46, 50, 97
Klal Israel (all of Israel), 123
Kol Nidrei (prayer), 116, 117

language. See theological language, in Levinas's work
Lanzmann, Claude, 62
Laozi, 42
law: and God, 33; Levinas's ethics vs., 51; and the other, 33, 35
Leibowitz, Yeshayahu, xi, 32
Le Pen, Jean-Marie, 21, 21n
Levi, Primo, 155
Leviticus, book of, 116, 124, 131, 138
Levi-Yitzhak, Rabbi, 146
Lévy, Benny, xv, 60–67
liberty, 134
Libya, 19
logic, 27, 34, 50
love: Levinas's notion of, 5–6; philosophy and, 52, 92, 106–07; significance of, 8–9; time and, 28. See also Eros
Lustiger, Jean-Marie, 159
Lyotard, Jean-François, 4, 45

Index   173

Maimonides, Moses, 134n1
Malraux, André, ix, xv, 3, 63–64, 71–90; *The Intemporal,* 80; *Israël,* 64; *Lazarus,* 71, 73, 76–79, 82, 84; *Man's Fate,* 77; *The Metamorphosis of the Gods,* 7; *The Mirror of Limbo,* 76, 78, 83; *Precarious Man and Literature,* 76, 87; *The Royal Way,* 70; *The Temptation of the West,* 87; *The Voices of Silence,* 80; *The Walnut Trees of Altenburg,* 80–82
Mao Zedong, 93
Marcel, Gabriel, 53
Marchais, Georges, 20, 20n
Marion, Jean-Luc, 4, 98
Maritain, Jacques, 156
marranos, 117
Marx, Karl, 20
Marxism, 94
maternity, 48–50
meaning: death and, 48, 89–90; in Levinas's work, 45–46; of life, 89–90; Malraux and, 77; problem of, 58
Menasce, Jean de, 14, 14n2
Mencius, 44
Mendelssohn, Moses, *Jerusalem,* 33
Mephibosheth, 136
Merleau-Ponty, Maurice, 3
Messiah, the, 24–25, 159
messianism, 21, 61, 67–68
metaphysics: defined, 104; end of, 2; and human-God relationship, 8; Levinas's notion of, xiii, 2, 48, 51, 100, 107. *See also* ethics: as first philosophy
Midrash, 32, 134, 139
Mishnah, 150
mitzvah (commandment), 33, 35
Montaigne, Michel de, 38
morality, Levinas's ethics vs., 18, 36, 51
Moro, Vázquez, 14, 14n1
Moses, 25, 35, 82–83, 115, 145, 155
murder, 133–34, 140
Mussaf (service), 124, 125

Nasser, Gamal Abdel, 54
Nazism, 45, 80, 94, 99
need, 103
Neilah (service), 118, 125
Niemoller, Martin, 156
Nietzsche, Friedrich, 3
1968, events of, 100
Nobel Prize for Literature, 54
nothing: death and, 26–27, 70–71, 75; holiness and, 18, 22
Numbers, book of, 143

Of God Who Comes to Mind (Levinas), 33, 34, 47, 58, 107
On Escape (Levinas), xiii
ontology, Levinas's move beyond, 1, 45–47, 51, 94, 95, 98–99
original sin, 126
other, the: and exteriority, 100–01; for-the-other, 59; freedom and, 56–57; God revealed through, 86; and the Good, 50; humanism of, xvi, 109; humanity revealed through, 33, 36, 47, 79–80; law and, 33, 35; responsibility for, 36, 82, 100–01, 110; Sartre on, 55–57; significance of, 2–3, 86; transcendence revealed through, 82, 85, 104–05; in Western philosophical tradition, 98. *See also* face of the other
otherwise than being, 43–45, 47, 86, 94, 96
Otherwise Than Being or Beyond Essence (Levinas), xiii, 43–44, 46–47, 49–50, 58, 79, 86, 100, 107, 109–10
otherwise than thinking, 45, 50–51, 91–110

Palach, Jan, 100
Parmenides, 98
Pascal, Blaise, 8, 38, 42, 44, 46, 50, 95
Paul, Saint, 24
Pazzi, Rabbi Simeon b., 144
Péguy, Charles, 42
Petrarch, 38
philosophers, responsibility of, 17

philosophy: and breach in Western philosophical tradition, xii, xiii, 45, 51, 91–110; etymology of, 92; and feelings, 91; and holiness, 108; Judaism and, 107; limits of, 96–97; and love, 52, 92, 106–07; and the other, 103; and thinking, 91–92
Picon, Gaëtan, 88
Plato, 7, 50, 92, 95–96; *Gorgias,* 44; *Phaedrus,* 93; *Republic,* 51
Poland, 31–32
politics, conditions for, 18
"Politics After!" (Levinas), 55
post-Christian Judaism, xii, 13–14
Prague Spring, 100
present, the, 55
progress, 20
prophets, 7, 96
Proust, Marcel, 35
pshat (literal meaning), 131
Pushkin, Alexander, 38

Raba, 136
rabbinical courts, 130
Rashi, 126–27, 131, 133, 135, 141–42, 144
Rawls, John, 3
reciprocity, 4–5, 22. See also human relations
Reflections on the Philosophy of Hitlerism (Levinas), 94
religion: and death, 69–71; impossibility of a world without, 66; Levinas's relation to, xv, 76, 84, 87–88; Levinas's theological language, xiii–xiv, 7, 46, 48–49, 101, 103
Ren, 50
repentance, 119, 122, 129–30, 140, 147, 150
responsibility: death and, 27; for evil, 134–35; holiness and, 17; and hostage, 23, 36–37; Judaism and, 115–16, 120; for the other, 36, 82, 100–01, 110; for other's wrongdoing, 106; philosophers and, 17; significance of, 34, 49–50; and transcendence, 82; unfairness and, 36
resurrection, 60, 67, 69–71, 81

revelation. See epiphany
Rey, Jean-François, 105
Ricoeur, Paul, xi, 3, 4–5, 21–23, 45, 50, 99, 105, 109; *Oneself as Another,* 4, 99
Rinser, Luise, 157–58
Roberts, Jill, *Is It Righteous to Be?,* ix
Rolland, Jacques, *Parcours de l'autrement,* 51
Rosenzweig, Franz, 41, 63, 72, 99, 119
Rosh Hashanah, xv, 113–16, 122, 126, 140
Rottenberg, Rabbi Hayyim Yaakov, 123–24
Rwanda, 80, 93

sacrifice: as absolute value, 9; God and, 8, 16; hostage and, 23–24; limits of, 29–30; and transcendence, 47; Warsaw Ghetto uprising as, 31. See also dying for; substitution
Sadat, Anwar al-, 55
Saint Cheron, Michaël de, ix–xii
Saint-John Perse (pseudonym of Alexis Léger), 84
Samuel, 15
Sanhedrin, 137, 141
sargueness (kittel) (mortuary costume), 120
Sartre, Jean-Paul, xiv–xv, 3–4, 43, 53–68, 88–89; *Anti-Semite and Jew,* 62; *Being and Nothingness,* 56, 59; *Hope Now,* 60; and the Jews, 60–68; and Kafka, 57–59; Levinas and, 53–55; Levinas on, 53, 55–56, 65–67; *Nausea,* 53–54
Satan, 25
Saul, 15, 136
scapegoat, 124
Schwabe, Moshe, 37–38
Senghor, Léopold Sédar, 155
Shakespeare, William, 38
Shekhinah (Presence of God), 118
Shoah, xii, 8, 32, 34, 43–45, 59, 77, 93, 99, 109, 134, 145, 149–61
sin, 126–27

Sodom, 123
Song of Songs, 5–6
Soviet Union, 93, 94, 100
Spinoza, Baruch, 101, 109–10
spirit, time and, 28
Stalinism, 45, 93, 94, 99
state, the, 17–18
Steiner, George, 24, 145
subjectivity: Levinas's notion of, 102; Proust and, 35–36. *See also* intersubjectivity
substitution, 34, 47, 49, 105–06, 109. *See also* sacrifice

tallith (prayer shawl), 120
Talmud, xv, 25, 29, 32, 68, 87, 128–31, 141, 143–44
Talmudic Readings (Levinas), 42
Tarfon, Rabbi, 137, 141
tchouvah (repentance), 119, 122, 140, 147. *See also* repentance
tefillah (prayer), 32, 122, 140
theological language, in Levinas's work, xiii–xiv, 7, 46, 48–49, 101, 103
Theory of Intuition in Husserl's Phenomenology, The (Levinas), xiv, 54
thinking, 91–92. *See also* otherwise than thinking
third, the: death and, 26–27, 75–76; face of the other and, 34; forgiveness and, 123, 161; God and, 34, 35; and human collectivity, 34; justice and, 106; logic and, 27, 34; and the state, 18
time: death and, 88; ethics and, 8; and the feminine, 29; Levinas's notion of, 27–28, 94; love and, 28; orientation of, 20–21, 61; and the present, 55. *See also* history
Time and the Other (Levinas), 29, 55, 98
Tolstoy, Leo, 8
Torah, 13, 15, 25–26, 35, 87, 114, 123–24, 126, 135, 137, 141, 143–44, 160
totality: critique of, 61, 63, 72, 95, 99, 102

Totality and Infinity (Levinas), xiii–xiv, 46, 49, 51, 56, 63, 79, 85, 87, 88, 99–100, 102, 104, 106
Touvier, Paul, 19, xii*n*
"Toward the Other" (Levinas), xv
Tractate Makkoth, 137
Tractate Megillah, 136
Tractate Rosh Hashanah, 30*n*, 113, 130–31
Tractate Sanhedrin, 68, 115, 124
Tractate Shabbath, 25
Tractate Yebamoth, 136
Tractate Yoma, 32, 127–29, 138, 139, 157
transcendence: agnosticism and, 74–75, 84; and being, 43; and immanence, 33; intersubjectivity and, 102; Levinas's notion of, 3, 86; and the other, 82, 85, 104–05; sacrifice and, 47. *See also* God
tsimtsoum, 119
twentieth century, xii, xvi, 11, 19–21, 109

universality, Judaism and, 114–16, 120

vengeance, 135–36
Viduy (Confession of Sins), 121
Villani, Sergio, 78
violence of the sacred, 87–88
Volozhiner, Rabbi Hayyim, 130

Warsaw Ghetto uprising, 31
Way, the, 42
Weil, Simone, 41
Western culture, 37–38
Western philosophical tradition, xii, xiii, 45, 51, 91–110
Wiesel, Elie, x, 146, 159
Wiesenthal, Simon, *The Sunflower,* xv–xvi, 150–58
woman. *See* feminine, the

Yom Kippur, xv, 113, 115–25, 129, 138–40, 142
Yugoslavia, 80

zdakah (charity), 122, 140
Zionism, xiii, 15–16, 21